This is a great book. It combines inspiring stories, documented research and practical strategies for creating real happiness in your life. I highly recommend this book.
~ Jack Canfield, Co-Author of Chicken Soup for the Soul°

Dr. Lombardo is my head coach for happiness!
~ Shaquille O'Neal, Four Time NBA Champion

A Happy You strikes a powerful chord both in its title and on every page: Happy and You go together. Dr. Lombardo's prescription for happiness empowers readers to make happiness a way of life and not some vague destination. The good doctor follows her own advice too. Reading her book will put you in a better mood. Can you ask for a better starting place on a journey to put more joy in your life?
~ Gerry Sandusky, Two-time Emmy winner

This is a book for everyone . . . eminently readable and bursting with profound advice.
~ Dr. Brian Latell, Author of "After Fidel" & Senior Research Associate, University of Miami

Elizabeth Lombardo prescribes psychological success, making it as simple as ABC. Dr. Lombardo has written a book that allows us to understand our feelings so we all can function better in life. This is a psychologist who can break down theory into practice. It makes each of us a better person. A dose of A *Happy You, Your Prescription for Happiness* will help you to create a more joyful you.
~ Daniel Benson M.D., Professor of Orthopedic Surgery University of California, Davis

Happiness inspires creative thinking and creative thinking inspires us to look for ways to look at life differently. Let Dr. Lombardo help you find a better life. I highly recommend this book!
~ Jeff Tobe, Professional speaker & best selling author of "Coloring Outside The Lines"

Wow! What a refreshing perspective on our life's pursuit of true happiness. *A Happy You* is more than the ABC's, it's the reminder each of us periodically needs to refocus on our mind and body. Each chapter and its prescription provide wise lessons. Dr. Lombardo's practical sense on internal examination doesn't include anesthesia, just desire. Sign up and experience a happy you!
~ John S. Haslett, President of The Haslett Management Group, Inc.

Happiness often seems like an elusive butterfly - here for a fleeting moment and then disappears. Thank you Elizabeth for taking the time to give us a step-by-step prescription for keeping our lives joyous each and every day. The truth is happiness is an inside job so do yourself a favor - read this book and start the journey.
~ Linda Franklin, The Real Cougar Woman.Com & author of "Don't Ever Call Me Ma'am"

A Happy You is a gift. It's a clear, complete and utterly usable presentation of the latest in positive psychology. Dr. Lombardo provides real-life examples throughout that leave even the skeptical reader no excuses. The author practices what she preaches, and her life bears the vibrant fruit of it. A Happy You lets you in on her secret. I'll be recommending this book to clients, family and friends.
~ Berit Johnson, PhD, Clinical psychologist in private practice

Dr. Lombardo's book *A Happy You: Your Ultimate Prescription for Happiness* encapsulates what it means to bring happiness to yourself by a simple, yet profound, alphabet of ideas. I remember a poster on the wall of my Mother's office that read "It's not the mountains ahead that wear you out, it's the grain of sand in your shoe." This book is certainly the Rx to help anyone take out the sand. This enlightening book should be a gift for anyone wanting to find their own best happiness. Well said and well done, Dr. Lombardo – the examples in this book are inspirational.
~ Mary E. Kier, Vice Chairman of Cook Associates, Inc

Dr. Lombardo provides the perfect prescription for happiness that can work for everyone. I'm POSITIVE it can help you, regardless of what is going on in your life.
~ Howard Cohen, MD, Board certified in Psychiatry, Pain Medicine, Psychosomatic Medicine, Geriatric Psychiatry, & Addiction Psychiatry

Dr Lombardo's book is something that EVERYONE can relate to and will learn from. It is a great reminder of easy things we can all incorporate into our daily routines to live a happier life. I can't wait to share this book with all my girlfriends as well as my work colleagues!
~ Kimberly Rose, Wall Street Executive

As an oncology nurse *A Happy You* is a perfect prescription for my patients. Despite what life throws at you, you can feel joy and appreciation. Read this book if you are struggling with anything in your life. It WILL help you!
~ Heather McBrier, RN, Oncology Nurse

What a prescription…wish I could bottle it! *A Happy You* is a must read (and reread) manual for anyone who believes in common sense ideas to achieve inner peace and success.
~ Mary G. Butterfield, Owner, Butterfield Interiors

This is a must read! As a business owner in the weight loss industry for the last 10 years, I say WOW to the reality of truth in this book. I am recommending that all my staff and patients read it. This practical guide will help my patients trying to lose stick with their weight loss program, renew their spirit, develop inner self-confidence, and find true happiness and contentment in their lives. I wish I had this book years ago!
~ Pamela Chairvolotti, Physicians Weight Loss Centers

Dr. Lombardo goes straight to the heart of happiness with her insights and expertise. Anyone who wants a happier, healthier life should read this remarkable book.
~ Jackie Silver, founder and president, Aging Backwards, LLC

As a mother of 4, there is a lot of energy going on in my life. *A Happy You* helps me enjoy my children, give myself permission to take time for myself, and truly appreciate (rather than criticize) who I am as a mother. Every parent (and those with parents) will benefit from this book!
~ Brooke Harrell, Mom in Newton, MA

No matter who you are or where you are in life, you will benefit from *A Happy You*. Start applying Dr. Lombardo's timeless advice and reap the benefits immediately.
~ Richard E. Hamilton, Executive Vice President TEC Benefits

Dr. Lombardo's prescription for happiness is great for everyone. This book reads like a personal therapy session - a very common sense and conversational approach to finding one's personal happiness.
~ Sherry Jo Matt, Meeting planner & Mother of 2

As a medical professional, this is the **best** prescription I have ever seen! Very easy to read with so many relevant examples...a **must** read for everyone in search of happiness!
~ Patti Haslett RN, Reston, VA

A Happy You is a simple, yet effective tool to guide you to a place of joy and peace. Lead the life of your dreams and all your relationships will prosper as well!
~ Kelly Schweiger, Owner Tomorrow's Employment Concepts, LLC & Mom of 2

A Happy You is the perfect combination of education, inspiration and exhilaration. Get this book for yourself and everyone you love.
~ Nicole Witt, Executive Director, The Adoption Consultancy

Insightful, practical and easy. Everyone...really everyone should read this book!
~ Joseph Onesta, Professional Speaker

This book gently teaches you how to find happiness within yourself, within your life... *A Happy You* will remind you how to find joy in everyday things, and really lift your spirits
~ Tricia Donalty Landi, Medical Sales Manager

A Happy You:

Your Ultimate Prescription for Happiness

By
Elizabeth Lombardo, Ph.D.

New York

A Happy You
Your Ultimate Prescription for Happiness

ISBN 978-1-60037-532-3

Library of Congress Control Number: 2009930599

MORGAN · JAMES
THE ENTREPRENEURIAL PUBLISHER

Morgan James Publishing, LLC
1225 Franklin Ave., STE 325
Garden City, NY 11530-1693
Toll Free 800-485-4943
www.MorganJamesPublishing.com

In an effort to support local communities, raise awareness and funds, Morgan James Publishing donates one percent of all book sales for the life of each book to Habitat for Humanity. Get involved today, visit **www.HelpHabitatForHumanity.org**.

To Kelly and Gracie for helping me to discover a whole new level of happiness. I love you both so much.

APPRECIATION

Now that I've finished this book and am writing the appreciation, the one thing I'm appreciating more than anything is how much work has gone into this project.

Before beginning, I imagined everything would be easily wrapped up within a few months: it wasn't! I'm very glad I didn't realize, though, as I don't think I'd have the manuscript I do now if I'd fully considered how long the process would be.

Over the course of the project, I've been incredibly fortunate to work with so many people who have been so willing to help make this dream a reality. I am so appreciative of each and every one of you:

To friends and colleagues – the Bengis, Clarkson and Fleming families, Elizabeth Cowell, Brooke Harrell, Patti and John Haslett, Michelle Moll, Kimberly Rose, Karen Swanson and Nancy Vogler: thank you for doing everything you could to help me to succeed.

To all my friends at the Mom's Club, especially Kelly Schweiger, Sherry Jo Matt and Heather McBride: thank you for being such amazing, inspirational women.

To the folks at my office (yes, that means you, Kurt Schweiger!): thank you for keeping me in touch with humankind when I was locked in my office writing.

To my mentors, Drs. Arthur and Christine Nezu: thank you for being my role models in both the world of Psychology and in life.

To Bill Cashman: thank you for your patience in looking over my early (and rather dreadful!) drafts.

To the gang from Quantum Leap - including Steve and Bill Harrison, Nancy Ippoliti, Carla Douglin, Teri Hawkins, Dr. K, Stefan Swanepoel, Jackie Silver and Sandra Keros: thank you for being there when I needed your ongoing support and guidance!

To all my past and present clients: thank you for letting me learn more from you than you know and for keeping me amazed with how you improve your lives. I am particularly grateful and inspired by those who gave their examples to this book to help others find happiness.

To all whose stories are presented here: thank you for letting us learn from you and the challenges you have overcome. What an incredible inspiration you all are.

To my editor, Ashley Werner: thank you for tireless and passionate dedication to this manuscript. You pulled many all-nighters to help me get this completed, and I am deeply grateful.

To my family: thank you, Mom and Dad, for starting my life out with true happiness and for seeing that it's continued on such a joyous path. Martha, thank you for your incredible instrumental and emotional support. Yes, you are the best. And to the Lombardo clan - thanks for welcoming me into your happy family.

To my amazing husband, Jeffrey: thank you for the infinite encouragement and love you share with me every single day. I feel so blessed to have you in my life!

To all the people who were there but I've forgotten to list here: thank you for helping to make this project what it's become – your names are here in my heart even if not in my now-emptied mind (writing a book takes it out of you!).

Contents

Introduction:

YOUR PRESCRIPTION FOR HAPPINESS

> _Consumer Alert:_ _The following side effects have been observed as results of greater happiness: better relationships, improved health, less stress, higher levels of energy, more self-esteem, a greater sense of purpose and a longer, more prosperous life._

Do you want to be happier? I don't just mean "Mmm, this is an amazing chocolate chip cookie" happy. No, I'm talking about real happiness: true satisfaction, contentment and joy in your life.

If so, you're not alone. According to a recent Gallup poll, over one-hundred-and-fifty million Americans say they want greater happiness in their lives. But how can they possibly be happy? Financial strains, problems with marriages and children, loneliness, illnesses, past traumas, pressures about work or a lack of it, low self-esteem, losses of loved ones . . . many people's lives seem to be a knot of problems which is constantly getting tighter.

For relief, they may grab on to what they hope will bring them happiness: excessive eating, smoking, drinking, drug abuse, spending money, extra-marital affairs…but in the end, all these do is bring about greater discontentment.

If this sounds familiar to you, hold on and don't give up:

there *is* a better way. I'm here to tell you that you REALLY CAN BE HAPPY without the addictive or unhealthy "solutions" you may have tried before. Trust me – I've worked with hundreds of clients over the past decade and I've seen it happen over and over again.

A great piece of news on the road to happiness is that it's more about what's going on inside your brain than what's going on outside of it. This often gets overlooked, but means it's possible to be full of joy and gratitude despite life's struggles!

Happiness depends more on the inward disposition of mind than on outward circumstances.

**- Benjamin Franklin,
An American Founding Father**

Dr. Mehmet Oz, when talking on the Oprah Winfrey Show about his vast experience of helping others, said he learned that instead of always needing medical intervention, "The *message* is the medicine." What follows in this book is that message. I call it your **ultimate happiness prescription.**

If you've spent your life looking for a happiness pill, your search ends here: I have your happiness prescription, and you don't need to go to the pharmacy to get it filled.

Your Happiness Prescription

As both a clinical psychologist and a physical therapist, I help patients pinpoint their problems and then prescribe what they need to do to overcome them. Using research from cognitive behavioral therapy and positive psychology as well as my personal and professional experiences, I've developed the ultimate happiness prescription.

Think things in your life are too stressful to let you be happy? Let me tell you about Roger.

Roger was referred to the Psychology Department where I worked because of a life-threatening injury sustained on his job as an electrician. A high-voltage electric shock had gone through both his arms, which were now so severely burned that the doctors had to amputate them in order to save his life.

Here was a man who had been working with his hands since he was twelve years old doing a job he adored. Now he had no arms— no fingers to adjust wires, no hands for feeding himself and no arms for hugging his children.

Before I first met him, I expected to find him feeling down in the dumps. Instead, I discovered a stunning example of the nature of true happiness.

You see, he was firmly convinced that his arms had been lost and his life saved for a reason. He didn't know exactly what it was, but each day he woke up with a fervent desire to experience his new life, to discover how to make a difference and to experience each and every breath as a gift.

He wasn't as ecstatic as a child given freedom in a candy store, of course, but he was definitely happy. He was grateful to be alive and was eager to see what his new life had to offer.

Roger's story demonstrates a vital component of happiness:

No matter what your circumstances, *you have complete control* of your own contentment. You don't need luck, other people or magic chemicals to feel happy and satisfied.[1]

Most of us don't live with tragedies like Roger's, but we all still experience stress and discontentment. Fortunately, there are sure ways to overcome these.

If you follow the instructions in this book, the first thing you'll realize is that genuine joy doesn't come from a band-aid of superficial pleasures (being skinnier, more beautiful, richer etc.). In fact, even people who win millions of dollars in the lottery return to their pre-win levels of happiness within a few months.

Interestingly, the same is true for people who have something severe happen in their lives. Usually within a couple of months their distress decreases and they're back to their normal happiness levels.

True happiness is about enjoying deeper, intangible experiences: friends, family, the use of your strengths, the application of your values and an appreciation for everything that's going on *right now*.

Happiness Doesn't Mean Always Being Happy

The truly happy person understands a great paradox: that it's okay, and even necessary, to occasionally be sad, upset or frustrated. Part of being happy is allowing yourself to experience these not-so-pleasant feelings. Instead of avoiding them, joyful people acknowledge that they happen, then stay hopeful while figuring out a solution.

---

1   People with clinical depression may need external assistance from mental health professionals to decrease depression and enhance happiness. If this is you, please know that: (1) You CAN get better with proper intervention, and (2) The tools in this book will certainly help you on that path.

In this book, you will see this great truth at work: the chapters will cause you a wide range of both positive and negative emotions, and in the end you'll have more gratitude and satisfaction because of it.

I'm sure you want to be more genuinely joyful, and I'm also sure that you want to be the one your friends turn to when they need a lift. You are not alone in wanting this, and you're in luck: by finding this book and starting to read it, you've taken the first step toward your new, happier life!

Happiness Is Like Playing Golf

Not all of us can be as good as Tiger Woods on the golf course; by the time he was two, he was already wowing spectators with his golfing prowess. What he also does, though, is practice. Despite his natural gifts, Tiger practices incessantly and can often be found for hours on the driving range the morning before a big tournament.

We can all take a lesson from this: skills get better with practice. This can be done to become a better golfer, but it can also be done to improve our happiness – which is where your ultimate happiness prescription comes in.

Regardless of where your happiness level is right now, you can achieve and maintain a completely new level of contentment. Best of all, you'll find everything you need to do this right here in this book.

How To Use Your Happiness Prescription

A Happy You is your ultimate Rx in alphabetical order; each chapter takes a different letter to correspond to specific actions you can take to fill your happiness prescription. I have included many examples of people just like you who are seeking and finding true happiness. Though I have changed some of their names to protect their privacy, each and every story is true.

You can read, explore and benefit from this book in any order you like: read the chapters alphabetically, or spice things up a little by first reading the ones which spell your name, your partner's name or your favorite team's name. Alternatively, just scan the titles and see which ones shout, "You need to read me right now!"

The order you read them really doesn't matter because each one has unique content. You'll need all the different components of your prescription at different times, but for now feel free to pick and choose as you like.

Your Happiness Assessment

Before you start enhancing your happiness, let's get a baseline level of your current contentment by taking the quiz below - or by going online to take it at www.ahappyyou.com. Just pick the options that best describe you most of the time:

1. How do you rate your level of joy?
   A. Overall, I'm very joyous and satisfied with my life.
   B. I'll be happier when things get better.

2. Overall, how do you view yourself?
   A. I believe in myself despite my faults.
   B. I feel that I'm a big loser.

3. What's your circle of friends most like?
   A. I've got at least two people I can rely on completely.
   B. I've got various acquaintances but no one who really knows me.

4. How would you define "being a good friend"?
   A. Spending quality time and lending an ear whenever needed.
   B. Sending out holiday cards and calling on friends' birthdays.

5. Overall, what kinds of goals do you have?
   A. My goals reflect my values and spirituality.
   B. My goals are to make as much money as I can and to retire early.

6. What occupies your daily thoughts?
   A. Consciously identifying positives in my life and in other people.
   B. Seeing negative aspects that must change to allow me to be happy.

7. What is your attitude toward volunteering?
   A. I don't volunteer as much as I'd like to, but I do what I can when I can.
   B. I give blood once a year at work.

8. How would you describe your career (being a stay-at-home mom IS a career)?
   A. I'm happy with my career choice for the most part.
   B. I work *two jobs*: what career?

9. How do you define creativity?
   A. Being able to change my routine now and then by trying something different.
   B. The ability to paint, draw or play a musical instrument (none of which I do).

10. How often do you take time out for yourself?
    A. I make sure I have some "me time" every week.
    B. I wish I had a second to myself.

11. When something bad happens in your life, what's your most common reaction?
    A. I try to change what I can, accept what I can't and use the entire experience as a learning opportunity.
    B. I lament over what should have been done to prevent the situation.

Your Happiness Score

If you got more B answers than A answers, you came to the right place! Your happiness prescription is here to provide you with a more fulfilling life.

If you got more A answers than B answers, that's great, but your work isn't complete. Any score below a seven indicates that you still have some areas you can work on to get even happier.

If you got eight or more A answers, good for you! Use the prescription to further strengthen the happiness habits you already have.

No matter where you are right now, the following chapters will teach you how to lead a happier, more fulfilling life.

Nothing can bring you happiness but yourself.

**—Ralph Waldo Emerson,
Poet and Philosopher**

A: APPRECIATION

APPRECIATE AND BE GRATEFUL FOR WHAT YOU HAVE

> **If you lost it all tomorrow,**
> **what would you miss most about today?**

Ever think happy people are just people who have no problems? Or that maybe they're delusional about life's real stresses?

In reality, neither is true. People who are happy experience pretty much the same frequency and seriousness of difficulties as everyone else (and their rate of psychosis is no higher, either).

One thing that is different, however, is their ability to appreciate things. While happy people haven't necessarily led an easy life or avoided the problems the rest of us face, they do make the most out of their circumstances: they see the positives even when there are many negatives.

Happy people also *truly appreciate the small things* (listening to a favorite song or watching a sunset, for example), and are even grateful for the lessons they learn from difficult experiences. We certainly saw this in the introduction with Roger and his life-changing experience.

The Diagnosis: Wearing negativity blinders

I had the blues because I had no shoes - until upon the street I met a man who had no feet.

- Dale Carnegie, Author and Speaker

Ask yourself the following question: if an impoverished man from a third-world country accompanied you for a day, what would he appreciate most that you take for granted? Perhaps it'd be clean drinking water? Maybe the freedom to choose your own friends and follow your own dreams? Could it be a closet full of clothes or indoor plumbing? Finding answers to this question is a way to appreciate what you already have – and to expose your **negativity blinders**.

An example of a negativity blinder would be if the impoverished man accompanied you and said, "Yeah you have a car, but it's not a luxury model." Instead of focusing on the positives of the situation, he'd be focusing on the negatives. Sadly, many of us have exactly this kind of thought process throughout our day-to-day lives.

What the impoverished man would be far more likely to say would be something like, "I can't believe you have your own car to use to go wherever you want, whenever you want!" *That's* appreciation (by the way, when was the last time *you* appreciated your car?).

Start appreciating the good things about your life right now. There's really no reason not to: they're all ready and waiting to be enjoyed! I'm not suggesting you totally blank out all your life's negative aspects, of course, but be sure to make the best of the good stuff.

Consider the following letter, which shows how one person (the mistress) can appreciate so many things missed by another (the wife):

Letter written from a mistress to a wife

How can you feel about your husband the way you do?

What you see is someone who has a pudgy middle.
But I see a man who has a warm smile.

What you see is someone who comes home late.
But I see a man who works hard trying to support his family.

What you see is someone who doesn't help around the house.
But I see a man who needs some rest and wishes you would sit down with him on the couch.

What you see is someone who burned dinner.
But I see a man who tried his best to let you relax.

What you see is someone who lets the kids run wild.
But I see a man who wants so badly to give you a much-needed break.

I am so envious of how much he loves you and am so amazed at how blind you are not to see it.

Sincerely,
The mistress

Your Prescription: Be thankful

If you don't think every day is a good day,
just try missing one.

- Cavett Robert,
Attorney and Founder of
The National Speaker's Association

The following suggestions will help you to uncover and appreciate the good that already exists in your life – leading you to greater happiness.

1. Start a gratitude journal. A gratitude journal is a document where you record experiences in your life that you feel grateful for and appreciate. These could be specific events, or just wonderful things that happen regularly.

Add three things to the list each day (even when you have a bad day!), and over time you'll develop a list of all the brilliant experiences and people you have in your life right now.

Some examples might include:

- ✓ A good night's sleep
- ✓ A workout when you really pushed yourself
- ✓ Spending time with a good friend
- ✓ Being productive at work/home
- ✓ Your spouse doing the dishes
- ✓ Hearing a child giggle
- ✓ Having a good meal
- ✓ Getting to work/home on time
- ✓ A good cup of coffee in the morning
- ✓ Having the support of family and friends

Sound a little too "peace-love-granola-y" to you? What if you suddenly lost your ability to move? What would you pine for most? After sustaining his spinal cord injury, Christopher Reeve said what he missed most was, "to be able to put my arms around my son." Consider yourself in his position: what would you long to do? Now start being grateful that you *can* still enjoy those experiences.

2. Take off the negativity blinders. When a negative event happens, stop and identify something positive that's also happening. For example, when my two-year-old or four-year-old (actually, often my two-year-old *and* my four-year-old) have a temper tantrum, I try to focus on the positives, such as: (1) I'm practicing good parenting by not giving in and/or (2) in ten years I'm going to *wish* temper tantrums were the worst of their behavior.

Challenge yourself to find at least one thing that's good, regardless of how small it might be. You might be amazed at how this initially awkward task becomes more automatic the more you practice it. As you take off the negativity blinders, you'll come to enjoy greater happiness.

3. Share your appreciation. When was the last time you thanked someone? Not just for obvious events (like a stranger holding the door open for you), but also for more everyday happenings: a friend calling, a child following directions or a spouse completing a chore?

Expressing gratitude for what others do has a special power: it helps you to become more aware of the good that's right there in front of you. It also brings joy to the person being appreciated and, better yet, increases the likelihood of that person repeating their actions in the future.

A great activity to do as a family is developing a dinner table ritual where each person shares one event that he/she appreciated about someone else at the table that day. Imagine what happy meals these would be!

In short, start enjoying what you already have in your life. As the singer and breast cancer survivor Sheryl Crow sings, "It's not having what you want. It's wanting what you've got."

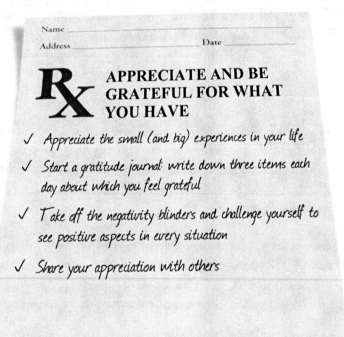

Name _____

Address _____ Date _____

R̶x APPRECIATE AND BE GRATEFUL FOR WHAT YOU HAVE

✓ Appreciate the small (and big) experiences in your life

✓ Start a gratitude journal: write down three items each day about which you feel grateful

✓ Take off the negativity blinders and challenge yourself to see positive aspects in every situation

✓ Share your appreciation with others

Signature _____

B: BELIEF

BELIEVE IN YOURSELF

> Even if you're not perfect, you can still believe in yourself — be confident in who and what you are on the inside.

We all know some negative people — the type who constantly find fault in others, always complain and who practically sap the positive energy out of us. In truth, these people are miserable in their own minds, too: they're full of negative beliefs about themselves and so have very low self-esteem.

Are you one of these people? What kinds of things do you say to yourself? Do you have negative thoughts echoing about in your head?

Whether you pay attention or not, your brain is constantly sending little messages to itself. Like mental "sticky notes," these set the tone for how you feel, how you interact with others and how you experience life. The biggest, brightest sticky notes are those which our brains send to us *about ourselves*.

Positive self-thoughts create self-confidence as we tackle life's challenges and lead to improved performance, more healthy behavior, less stress and greater happiness. Negative, self-defeating thoughts make us feel lousy. In my practice, I often see the results of this type of low self-esteem - such as:

- ✓ Overeating
- ✓ Failed relationships

7

- ✓ Poor job performance
- ✓ Depression
- ✓ Insomnia
- ✓ Procrastination
- ✓ Chronic pain
- ✓ Alcohol and drug abuse

A simple wisdom told to children often gets lost on adults: you need to believe in yourself. If you do, your actions, feelings and thoughts will reflect your new attitude. I'm not talking about an overly inflated sense of self-confidence or narcissism, of course, but it's definitely important to value who and what you are.

In order to take the steps toward happiness outlined in this book, you have to believe that you're worthy of being happy and that you have the ability (or are at least willing to try) to bring more happiness into your life. Believing in yourself is a vital component of **the happiness prescription**.

The Diagnosis: Low self-esteem

> *It's a simple message,*
> *And it comes straight from the heart:*
> *Believe in yourself,*
> *For that's the place to start.*
>
> **-From the Theme to**
> ***Arthur*, a Children's Show**

So, where's your level of self-confidence? Use a scale from 0 (not at all confident) to 10 (absolutely confident).

Ask yourself how much you:
- ✓ Believe in your own self-worth?
- ✓ Believe you can do what you set out to do?

Now ask yourself: how could you *increase* these numbers? It might surprise you that the most effective way to improve your confidence is not to change your external circumstances (by getting a higher paying job, for example), but to address your internal circumstances. This especially includes changing what you say to yourself about yourself.

Imagine what life would be like if you truly believed in everything you said and did. Would you have a go at something you'd always wanted to try? Would you stop drowning your sorrows in a bottle of wine or a plate full of cookies? Would you enjoy spending time with your friends and family more because you weren't picking at them for your own insecurities?

Tennis Hall of Famer Chris Evert once said, "In a decisive set, confidence is the difference." This applies to life off the court, too. Whatever your goal is (to lose weight, earn a degree, have a happy marriage etc.), statistics overwhelmingly show that those who believe in themselves are the ones who succeed.

Colonel Sanders is a good example of this: he tried to sell his chicken recipe at more than one thousand places before he found a buyer interested in his eleven herbs and spices. It took seven years for the seventy-five-year-old Colonel to sell his fried chicken company for a finger-lickin' $2 million.

Another example is Albert Einstein, who was made fun of as a child because of his dyslexia. He rarely spoke and had trouble with math, but he *did* believe in himself. He ultimately overcame his difficulties, went on to become one of the most brilliant scientists in history and was even named "Person of the Century" by Time Magazine.

Both of these individuals could have quit because of their initial failures, but instead chose to use their faith in themselves to propel them to achieve goals beyond their wildest dreams. Life can be challenging, but believing in yourself will help motivate you to fulfill your aspirations and to be happy.

Your Prescription: Enhance your self-confidence

A man cannot be comfortable without his own approval.

-Mark Twain,
Author and Humorist

Coming up with positive thoughts about yourself is one thing, but actually believing those thoughts might seem like another challenge altogether.

To think of it another way, our thoughts are like songs. When you first hear a song, can you sing all the words? Of course not. The more you hear the song, however, the more you're able to sing along with it. Eventually you can screech the words at the top of your lungs in the shower without even having the song played (okay, I may be disclosing too much about myself here!).

Like a song, the more you hear and recite positive statements about yourself, the more you internalize them and the more you come to truly believe them. Here are some hints to help you to accomplish this:

1. Develop a list of affirmations. Close your eyes and consider the following: if you were an author writing a story about the ideal you, how would you describe yourself? What kind of person would you want to be? What kinds of thoughts would you like to have about yourself? Write these down and recite them aloud daily.

Here are some examples to consider:

✓ I accept myself for who I am
✓ I love myself - flaws and all
✓ I can do this
✓ I'm proud of myself for my past accomplishments
✓ I'm proud of myself despite my past

Remember - the more you hear something, the more that concept becomes internalized. This is true whether the primary source is you (via your self-talk) or someone else.

Hilary Swank is a great example of this. Growing up with her family in a Washington trailer park, she was ostracized by the more affluent families at her school. She found comfort in the fantasies of books and movies. At the age of ten she performed in her first play and discovered her love for acting.

When she was fifteen, her parents divorced, and soon after her mother took her to Los Angeles to pursue a career in acting. With almost no money and no job there, she was going on faith in her daughter alone.

Eventually Hilary got hired as an actress. She played various parts in television shows - culminating in the hit Beverly Hills 90210. *After she was on for only fourteen episodes, though, the show was canceled. But she remained persistent and gained her next role as the lead character in* Boys Don't Cry, *which landed her the first of her two Oscar awards.*

When asked about her success, she's said, "I didn't have formal acting training. I just had my mom who believed in me." This confidence her mom had in her is what Hilary adopted in herself.

She now takes on challenges such as non-traditional roles in films that others without her self-confidence might avoid. As acclaimed English author Samuel Johnson said, "Self-confidence is the first requisite to great undertakings."

Hilary's self-assurance is also a motivating factor in her reaching out to others. As an example, she traveled to India in 2006 to volunteer with young children. "The poverty is rampant," she described, "but they are some of the happiest people I've ever met. I saw plenty of barefoot kids with nothing who were happy. It's a reminder of what's important in life - family, health and being able to have a place to go where you can learn and stretch your mind."

When you believe in yourself like Hilary Swank does, you give yourself permission to try new and rewarding adventures. Self-confidence also takes away the stress of beating yourself up - allowing you to enjoy the experiences that you have.

2. Act as if you believe in yourself. Walk tall and proud even if that's not how you're feeling inside: the more you do it, the greater the confidence you'll feel. Next time you're going into a big meeting feeling scared and overwhelmed, walk in with a spring in your step or a swagger of self-assurance. It'll really help you to better believe in yourself.

Another way to act with self-confidence is to accept compliments: just say "thank you" when someone has something nice to say. Even if you don't 100% believe in it, remember that beauty is in the eye of the beholder.

3. Stop the (insane) comparisons. There's always going to be someone faster, richer, skinnier, prettier, sexier or smarter than you. It's a fact of life – but so what? You're the best *you* out there. No one brings the same unique combination of strengths, abilities and passions to the world.

If you spend all your time focusing on why other people are better than you, you'll never be able to truly believe in yourself and be grateful for the wonderful qualities that make you who you are.

A participant at a workshop I was once giving offered the following metaphor:

"If you're running in a race, you can compare yourself to all those ahead of you - or you can turn around, see the people behind you and realize that you're not actually doing that badly. It's not that you're any better than any of the people behind you (or those people sitting at home on the couch), but it can help you to feel more confident about what you're doing. Just be proud that you're out there trying – whether it's in a race or in life."

How can you use this concept in your life to put more belief into what you do – regardless of the outcome? Believing in yourself is an essential step toward achieving happiness.

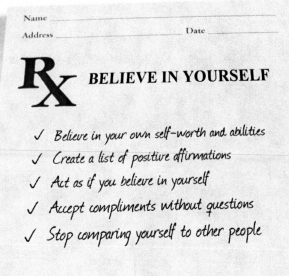

Name _____

Address _____ Date _____

Rₓ BELIEVE IN YOURSELF

✓ Believe in your own self-worth and abilities

✓ Create a list of positive affirmations

✓ Act as if you believe in yourself

✓ Accept compliments without questions

✓ Stop comparing yourself to other people

Signature _____

C: CREATIVITY

USE CREATIVITY TO BRING CONTENTMENT

> Creativity gives you the ability to be happy in ways you may never have dreamed possible.

Creativity requires imagination, innovation, inspiration and often unconventionality, and refers to making, inventing or producing something new. This could be an idea, an object, an approach to a situation or a work of art: the power creativity holds is virtually limitless.

Soon after breaking a world record by winning an eighth gold medal in a single Olympics, Michael Phelps attributed his unparalleled success to his creative approach. He said, "nothing is impossible. With so many people saying it couldn't be done, all it takes is imagination."

Many sports figures and other successful individuals talk about being "in the zone" when they're performing at their best: completely focused, productive and adaptive to whatever challenges are thrown at them. Their creativity is at a peak. Mihaly Csikszentmihalyi, a world-renowned researcher on creativity, has a name for this: **flow**.

Not just experienced by athletes, flow is a state of optimal experience, high concentration and initiative. When people are in flow-type experiences, they're fully engaged and creative. Time seems to slip away; they focus on and enjoy only what they're experiencing at that specific moment.

Have you ever experienced flow? If so, how did it feel? As Dr. Csikszentmihalyi claims, for most of us, "a typical day is full of anxiety and boredom," but "flow experiences provide the flashes of intense living against this dull background." In other words, engaging in creative activities that help you to find flow is a way of bringing more happiness into your life.

The Diagnosis: Stuck in a rut

> *If at first the idea is not absurd,*
> *there is no hope for it.*
>
> **-Albert Einstein,**
> **Theoretical Physicist**

If you're often bored and feel stuck in the doldrums of a monotonous daily routine, you might be suffering from a lack of creativity in your life.

Many of us confuse "creativity" with being "artistic," but in reality, you don't have to be able to play an instrument or draw to be creative. A creative person is simply someone who comes up with original ideas, which is something everyone can do.

Christine Holton Cashen is a Certified Speaking Professional who helps people around the world become more creative.[2] She believes, "everyone is creative, but we forget how to use it. In fact, we are educated *out* of creativity in school when we are taught to memorize the one right answer rather than use our imagination and innovation." Luckily, it can be re-learned.

Being creative has many benefits. In general, creative people:

✓ Feel more self-confident
✓ Experience less stress and depression

---

2   For more information on Christine Holton Cashen, visit her website at www.adynamicspeaker.com.

✓ Have more funds in the bank because of their creative
   ways of making and saving money
✓ Find multiple fulfilling ways to spend their time rather
   than feeling stuck doing the same thing
✓ Are able to generate more happiness in their lives

Sadly, certain obstacles can hinder imagination and innovation, such as:

✓ Stress
✓ Forcing the creative process
✓ Fear
✓ Perfectionism
✓ Self-doubt
✓ Comparing your work or self to others
✓ Procrastination
✓ Not having enough "free" time

Don't let these hurdles prevent you from experiencing the joys of creativity: many people spend far too much time worrying about the outcome of their creative endeavors rather than enjoying the process itself. Your success with creativity isn't determined by the beauty of your drawing or the genius of your innovation, but rather by the happiness you experience while you're being creative.

Engaging in creative acts is a simple way to find peace in the midst of a hectic day, see events in a different light, experience stimulation in a less-than-exciting routine and increase your happiness.

Your Prescription: Flex your creative muscles

Happiness is not the mere possession of money; it lies in the joy of achievement and the thrill of creative effort.

-Franklin D. Roosevelt,
32nd President of the United States

Creativity is like a muscle that grows and flourishes when you exercise it. Conversely, it can shrink when you let your talents go to waste. In other words, the more you practice creativity (regardless of the outcome), the easier and more enjoyable being creative becomes.

Here are some guidelines to help tone your creative muscles:

1. Question the status quo. Strive to be curious in your everyday life: consider why things are performed in a certain way and how day-to-day processes work. If you're less than satisfied with what's going on, come up with different ways to make things better, more fun, more productive and more conducive to happiness.

This same concept applies to questioning how you view certain circumstances. In his book, *Coloring Outside the Lines*, Creativity Guru Jeff Tobe says, "you constantly have to look at situations from more than one perspective. When we see the world through 'their' (your spouse's, customer's or even foe's) eyes, it allows us to become less married to the circumstances. It may even make you smile." [3]

Consider Peter Shankman, an entrepreneur, Public Relations (PR) expert and adventurer who has changed the face of journalism with his innovative ideas. Th roughout his life, Peter has had Attention Deficit Hyperactivity Disorder which might hinder some, but by being creative, he's been able to find success and happiness.

Peter is the author of Can We Do Th at?! Outrageous PR Stunts Th at Work - And Why Your Company Needs Th em,

---

[3]   For more information on Jeff Tobe, visit his website at www.jefftobe.com.

which teaches companies how to use creativity to enhance their marketing. He further applied his novel thinking when he developed HelpAReporterOut.com.

The service originally started as a group on Facebook where journalists submitted requests for sources to be used on their assignments. Thousands of people looking for their fifteen minutes of fame responded. The group became so huge that Peter had to create a website, and after only one year, over seventy-thousand people had signed up to "help a reporter out."

The experts are happy to get media coverage and the journalists appreciate the ease of getting good sources. This innovative service is also free!

2. Schedule time to be creative and find your flow. Identify creative activities that you enjoy and schedule time for them. Set aside at least twenty minutes of uninterrupted time and see where your creativity takes you. You might be surprised at what you create and how you feel when you're doing it.

3. Set the mood. Certain environments are more conducive to creativity than others. For some, a quiet setting with soft candles gets the creative juices flowing. Others thrive in bright, energetic surroundings.

Depending on your personality and interests, outlets that spark your creativity might include being in nature, meditating, painting, drawing, writing, listening to music, dancing or just being downright silly.

4. Move your body. Physical movement helps increase oxygen delivered to the brain, which then generates enhanced brain activity and increased creativity. Moving in a repetitive manner (such as walking or biking) can stimulate creativity similar to meditation.

When I asked Peter Shankman how he stays so positive and motivated, he said, "Finding time to stop, stand up and do whatever it takes to generate a burst of creativity is a very overlooked necessity in our daily grind. Taking five minutes to walk up and down some stairs, forty-five minutes for a run or even thirty seconds to drop and do ten pushups radically alters your brain chemistry and gives you a massive creativity boost. I couldn't imagine a day without it." Why don't you give his suggestion a try?

Use creativity to escape from dullness and find innovative approaches in life to discover inner joy. Enjoy the satisfaction and happiness that wash over you as you let your creativity flow.

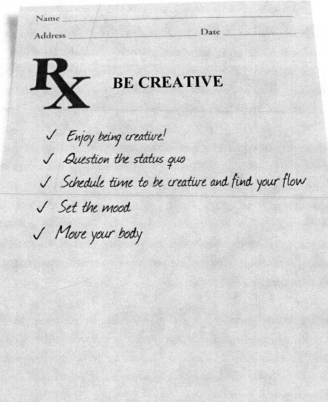

Name _____

Address _____ Date _____

R℞ BE CREATIVE

✓ Enjoy being creative!

✓ Question the status quo

✓ Schedule time to be creative and find your flow

✓ Set the mood

✓ Move your body

Signature _____

D: DEFINITIONS

OPTIMIZE HOW YOU DEFINE HAPPINESS

> You have complete control over how you define important variables in your life. Make them realistic, attainable and consistent with your values, and they'll bring you immense joy.

Your thoughts and the definitions they create about your life determine how you feel and what you do. By taking control of these perceptions, you can enhance your happiness.

Growing up as a young boy in Sydney, Australia, John Maclean always dreamed of being a professional athlete - specifically a football player. Sadly, his dreams were almost shattered when a truck hit him while he was out cycling one day, leaving both of his legs paralyzed. A paraplegic at the age of twenty-two, John entered into a period of self-pity and became convinced that his days of happiness were over.

In spite of his depression, as his rehabilitation progressed, he learned to redefine his situation. For example, he saw other patients with broken necks and began to appreciate the use of his upper body. He channeled his energy into accomplishing what he could do rather than focusing on what he couldn't. "The little boy was emerging inside me and wanted to continue his dream," he remembers.

In the years that followed, John became a world-renowned athlete. Among his amazing accomplishments, he completed the Gatorade

Ironman World Championship in 1997, represented his country in both the Olympics and the Paralympics in 2000 and became the first wheelchair athlete to swim the English Channel.

When asked for advice, he says that perspective is paramount: "Change will happen – it's how you deal with it that's important. You've got to believe in yourself, be with positive people, ask questions, ask for help if you need it and just have a go."

As events in your life change, you may need to modify your definitions to optimize your happiness and fulfill your dreams. Sadly, many of us are "closet perfectionists" - if not perfectionists outright. We have definitions of the ideal job, the ideal mate, the ideal house and the ideal car - even the ideal tennis partner or ideal dinner.

It's because of this perfectionist thinking that we come to see things as black and white: we get the notion that everything must be either "ideal" or "not worth having at all." We carry an underlying belief that if things and people in our lives (including ourselves) don't live up to our ideals, they're failures. This sets us up for disappointment, as there's a sense that "if my husband, job, life etc. aren't how I ideally define them, I'm doomed to being unhappy."

To further complicate matters, our definitions are individual and unique. Consider your definition of an ideal vacation, for example. For some, this might be lying in a hammock with nothing to do all day, whereas others would get bored *just thinking* about such leisureliness. For them, the perfect holiday might involve an adventure such as rock climbing, camping or bungee jumping. The definition of the "ideal," be it for a vacation or otherwise, depends on the individual.

Clearly we all have unique definitions about aspects of our lives, but problems can arise because we often don't evaluate how accurate or how helpful these definitions are. In fact, we're often not even aware of them. Despite this, it's quite common for our definitions to be major contributors to stress and discontent when our realities don't match up to our ideal expectations. The solution is to become *conscious* of our definitions to see whether they're helpful - or whether they're really just sources of angst.

The Diagnosis: Not being realistic

My definition of success is to live your life in a way that causes you to feel a ton of pleasure and very little pain.

-Tony Robbins,
International Best-Selling Author
and Motivational Speaker

We all have different personal definitions that go beyond textbook explanations. Consider your definition of:

- ✓ Success
- ✓ Failure
- ✓ The ideal mate
- ✓ The perfect co-worker
- ✓ A best friend
- ✓ Happiness

Sometimes our definitions about these can be accurate and helpful, but other times the opposite is true. When this is the case, they can lead to significant distress.

For example, if your definition of a good boss is someone who proactively offers you a raise without you asking for one, you may be sorely disappointed. A more helpful definition of a good boss might be something like, "Someone who provides constructive feedback, listens to my concerns and problem-solves issues with me."

While we don't always recognize our definitions, we become harshly aware of them when we or someone else deviates from them. To illustrate, have you ever been upset at someone such as a significant other – only to have him totally miss why you're reacting the way you are? Most likely all that has happened in this situation is that your partner has deviated from *your* definition of what is "okay" but not his.

Your Prescription: Redefine yourself

To freely bloom – that is my definition of success.

**-Gerry Spence,
Attorney and Writer**

The following steps will help you to redefine key variables in your life to experience greater happiness:

1. Identify your definitions. As mentioned before, we are often unaware of how we define our lives' variables until they're violated and so cause us distress. While they can sometimes be useful to us as well, however, the best way to deal with our definitions is to proactively determine how they're defined.

With this information, we can decide whether we need to change them, and if we do, how to best make the changes. To do this, first write down how you define a:

- ✓ Good friend
- ✓ Good parent
- ✓ Good child
- ✓ Good spouse
- ✓ Good employee

Now write down how you define these overriding variables:

- ✓ Success
- ✓ Happiness
- ✓ Purpose
- ✓ Love

2. Watch out for "should." The term "should" plays a big role in our definitions. Whenever you think, say or hear "should," recognize it like a trumpet sounding "da-da-dee-dum: this is my definition!"

Here are some common "shoulds" that I hear in my practice and their corresponding definitions:

"Should" Statement	Definition	Result
"I should be married by now."	Someone who's worthy and loveable is married; unmarried people are unworthy and unlovable	Poor self-esteem Focusing on the lack of a wedding ring rather than on enjoying current relationships
"She should know I'm down and need some support."	A good friend anticipates your every desire	Disappointment with a friend Argument or avoidance
"I should work out every day. I'm so lazy."	Someone really trying to be healthier works out daily	Guilt and increased stress (which ironically often lead to emotional eating)

3. Question your definitions. Next, review your definitions:

✓ Which characteristics are vital and which are nice but unnecessary?
✓ How do these definitions really work for you? Do they make you happier or more stressed?

✓ How do they work for your loved ones?

✓ Are they realistic and attainable?

✓ Do they set you up for success or disappointment?

4. Redefine definitions that are causing you unhappiness.
Make sure your definitions are:

✓ Consistent with your values

✓ Setting you up for success

✓ Criteria you can truly believe in

✓ Realistic and attainable

✓ Causing happiness by supporting positive feelings about yourself

Let's look at a specific example:

Peggy had three children younger than eight-years-old. She came to see me because she was feeling stressed out. "I feel like I'm going crazy," she said when I first saw her.

A stay-at-home mother, Peggy told me her definition of a good mom was someone who was always calm with her children, had a freshly cooked meal prepared on time each night and was there for them 24/7. While these are nice goals, this definition of a good mother is rather stringent and difficult (if not impossible) to consistently achieve. The outcome? Peggy was a good mom who beat herself up.

During our time together, she revised her definition of a good mother to be one who:

✓ *Loves her children unconditionally*

✓ *Teaches her children right from wrong (including apologies by Mom when she loses her cool)*

✓ *Ensures that her children are properly cared for (by herself, their father, their family or someone else she trusts)*

✓ *Takes care of her family as well as herself*

For any moms out there, how would these definitions work for you? For Peggy, they truly helped her transform her life: her self-

confidence grew and her stress levels dwindled. At the same time, she started to really enjoy being with her children because she was no longer overwhelmed by her previous self-criticalness.

The ultimate result? A happier Peggy and a happier family. You really can enhance your happiness by redefining damaging definitions.

Our definitions affect our happiness and our satisfaction with our partners, friends, family, careers and lives. If your definitions aren't working for you, change them - they belong only to you! Make certain you're not letting harmful definitions stand in the way of the happiness you deserve.

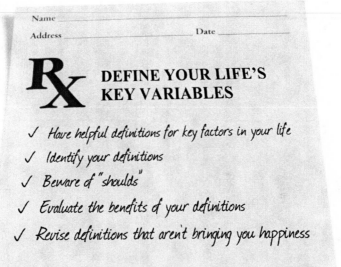

Name _____

Address _____ Date _____

R℞ DEFINE YOUR LIFE'S KEY VARIABLES

✓ Have helpful definitions for key factors in your life

✓ Identify your definitions

✓ Beware of "shoulds"

✓ Evaluate the benefits of your definitions

✓ Revise definitions that aren't bringing you happiness

Signature _____

E: EXERCISE

EXERCISE YOUR WAY TO HAPPINESS

> Exercise provides powerful benefits to your mind and body.

After ten years of being married, Joanne Giannini's husband wanted out - citing her almost 185 pound, 5'4" frame as a contributing factor. "I'm not attracted to you anymore," he said. Prior to this, Joanne had sensed that, "he wasn't crazy about the way I looked, which made me depressed." To cope with her depression, she had ironically ended up eating more.

Following his exodus, Joanne's depression accelerated to the point where she felt she could barely function. The anger and pain were essentially consuming her life. A month later, however, she "found some old exercise videos. I dusted one off and tried it out. My mind was so cluttered with anger and pain, and exercising washed it away. It felt unbelievably good to stomp my feet and clear my head."

Today, Joanne is 55 pounds lighter and continues to exercise regularly. As a result, her size and body composition have been transformed. While not as outwardly obvious, she's also experienced a huge transformation on the inside: her self-confidence, previously depleted, has strengthened and she has a lot more energy for enjoying her life. Joanne's happiness level is soaring, and it all started with exercise.

Most of us know about the benefits of exercise on our *physical health* - including weight loss, decreased blood pressure, improved "good" cholesterol, enhanced cardiovascular function and the prevention of certain chronic illnesses. As the 17th Earl of Derby once said, "Those who think they have no time for bodily exercise will sooner or later have to find time for illness."

Did you also know, though, that exercise is also good for your *psychological health*? Evidence shows that exercise:

- ✓ Raises mood-enhancing neurotransmitters in the brain
- ✓ Enhances positive attitudes
- ✓ Releases muscle tension
- ✓ Promotes better sleep
- ✓ Has a calming effect
- ✓ Lessens anxiety and depression

There have been some amazing studies looking into the benefits of exercise on depression. One of these involved over one-hundred-and-fifty people with severe depression who were randomly assigned to one of three treatments: (1) Anti-depressant medication, (2) Exercise or (3) Anti-depressant medication *and* exercise.

After four months of treatment, all three groups had similarly lower levels of depression, which showed exercise to be as effective as the anti-depressant medication. Pretty neat, huh?

What I think is even more amazing is that, after ten months of treatment, the groups performing exercise were doing significantly better than the medication-only group. In the long term, it appears that exercise can be even more powerful than anti-depressant medication for people suffering with depression.[4]

---

4   This is NOT to say that anti-depressant medications are useless or that, if you are on them, you should stop taking your pills and just exercise. Instead, anti-depressant medications can be an important component of an individual treatment plan that you and your healthcare provider choose together.

The Diagnosis: Inactivity

> *The perils of overwork are slight compared with the dangers of inactivity.*
>
> **-Thomas Edison,**
> **Inventor and Businessman**

According to the Centers for Disease Control, only 26% of Americans perform the prescribed thirty minutes of moderate exercise five days a week. In fact, the number of people who regularly exercise has not increased significantly over the last two decades - despite a greater national focus on the importance of the habit.

Our commercialized society has given many people the notion that, unless we follow the national exercise recommendations to the tee, buy all the latest workout equipment or have a membership at a health club, we're wasting our time.

The reality is that exercise doesn't have to be perfect or costly! All you have to do is make your goal to incorporate physical activity a regular and important part of your life. You'll be amazed at the power this can have on your mind and body. After all, aren't you worth it?

Your Prescription: Get started and stay motivated

> *The reason I exercise is for the quality of life I enjoy.*
>
> **-Dr. Kenneth H. Cooper,**
> **The Father of Aerobics**

The most frequently cited obstacles to exercise include it being boring, hard, and/or time consuming. However, it need not be any of these. By finding activities you actually enjoy, you'll see that exercise can actually be fun. Really!

Use the following tips to help incorporate exercise into your life and improve your happiness level as a result:

1. Find the right exercise program for you.[5] To help you find your best exercise routine, consider the following questions:

- ✓ What types of exercise/physical activities do you enjoy?
- ✓ What goals do you have in mind? Do you want to lose weight, be stronger, enhance your flexibility or improve your mood?
- ✓ Do you prefer to exercise with a group or alone?
- ✓ Do you have any physical conditions that restrict your exercise options?
- ✓ What programs are flexible enough to fit your schedule?

Remember, exercise comes in all shapes and forms; although jogging and pumping iron are traditional ways of being physically active, they're far from the only ones available. Find something you enjoy doing: dancing, playing with your children, taking your dog for a walk, jumping on a trampoline or playing a sport (regardless of how "good" you are at it).

Start slowly (maybe fifteen minutes of activity) and gradually increase the duration and/or intensity. Believe me - over time you'll actually look forward to doing these things!

When I was in high school, I used to joke that exercise was "against my religion." Even the thought of going for a jog induced a visceral response of overwhelming dread. In college, however, I made myself workout to try to prevent the Freshman 15. When my girlfriends went to aerobics classes, I would sometimes join them. As I continued, I really started to enjoy it.

The year I graduated, I actually became a Certified Group Fitness Instructor. Now I truly look forward to my Spinning® and kickboxing classes: the boost in energy and mood I get is amazing.

---

5   Check with your doctor before starting a new exercise program. This is especially important if you have a chronic health condition such as diabetes, heart disease or obesity.

2. Remember the benefits. Everybody has different goals in mind when they exercise, but whatever yours are, focus on *them* as your motivation to get moving. Write out the benefits you want to achieve from exercising, and then post them where they'll be easily visible (the bathroom mirror, the fridge etc.). Read them over daily and be proud of yourself for trying to achieve them.

3. Work exercise into your daily routine and commit to it. Schedule your workout just as you would a doctor's appointment or an important meeting - don't break it. Chose activities that are conducive to actually happening, too: joining a fitness club many miles from your home, for example, may not be your best option. Often the best solution is to stick to the simplest option available, so try just going outside and taking a walk.

4. Make it fun. Make your exercise time a fun time by trying the following:

- ✓ **Mix it up**: try different activities in different settings
- ✓ **Distract yourself**: get an MP3 player and load it with your favorite workout tunes or an audio book, or record your favorite TV shows and only let yourself watch them while you exercise
- ✓ **Find an exercise partner**: work out with another person who's committed to getting into shape. They - be it a friend, spouse or personal trainer - can give you boosts of motivation when you need them and make your workouts more fun

5. Never ignore pain. If your body aches from working out, this may not be a bad thing, but if you feel pain, stop exercising and rest - you could damage your joints and muscles by continuing. If you're getting persistent and/or severe pain, it's best to visit the doctor. Be sure to learn the difference between muscle soreness caused by training and sharp pain caused by injury early on.

When you exercise, your mind and body both enjoy the benefits. Be proud that you're investing time and energy into a healthier and happier you.

Name _____

Address _____ Date _____

℞ EXERCISE YOUR WAY TO HAPPINESS

✓ Start moving – it's good for your body and mind

✓ Do physical activities you enjoy

✓ Remember the benefits of exercise

✓ Incorporate exercise into your daily routine and commit to it

✓ Find ways to make exercise fun: try new activities, listen to music or find an exercise partner

✓ Never ignore pain

✓ Stay positive and be proud of yourself

Signature _____

F: FORGIVENESS

FORGIVE YOURSELF AND OTHERS

> Forgiveness is a gift you give to yourself that can transform your health, mood, self-esteem and relationships. It will set you free from the past and let you enjoy your present and future.

Forgiveness is about releasing anger and resentment against someone who has wronged you. Sometimes we need to forgive ourselves, and other times we need to forgive another person. Forgiveness is not always easy, but can be an incredibly powerful tool to creating happiness and inner peace. Take the story of Susan Lee-Titus:[6]

Susan was a successful and happy professional who furthered her love of aerobic dance by becoming a dance instructor. Life was good until the day two men exploded into her dance studio and raped her. She shares her experiences in her book The Dancer: From Victim to Victory.

Susan was brutally wounded in the attack both physically and emotionally, and what it followed was an eight-year process of draining physical and mental rehabilitation. Over the course of this time, she also undertook a spiritual journey.

---

6   Thanks to Susan for taking the time to speak with me. Learn more about her journey to forgiveness at www.thedancerreturns.com.

Despite experiencing posttraumatic stress disorder, Susan found renewed faith in the power of forgiveness. Instead of growing isolated, hostile and bitter by refusing to forgive the men who raped her, she eventually freed herself from her resentment. As a result of this forgiveness, her life has been transformed.

In addition to generating greater harmony in her own life, Susan also started The Joy Dancers. *This outreach program teaches incarcerated women how to release their anger through aerobic dance, and is particularly poignant as it allows her to help the same criminal element that harmed her. This act completes the circle of forgiveness.*

By learning to forgive, Susan has not only developed an inner peace, but has also learned the beauty of compassion that comes from helping other women in pain.

The Diagnosis: Holding a grudge

> *To forgive is to set a prisoner free and discover that the prisoner was you.*
>
> **-Lewis B. Smedes,**
> **Author, Ethicist and Theologian**

Think about any current resentment you have, and ask yourself: "Does holding this grudge make me feel any better about the pain this person has caused?"

Forgiveness is the antidote to the negative energy produced by holding a grudge. As one of my clients described it, "Forgiving has allowed me to put down that fifty pound weight I've been carrying around with me for years. Now I feel like I'm almost floating: I'm so free."

Forgiveness is important not only for major, life-altering offenses, but also for more minor inconveniences: a co-worker who's messed up a project; a spouse who's come home late; a friend who's forgotten to call you on your birthday. By releasing this resentment and stress, people who forgive are more likely to experience physical and psychological wellness, and also more happiness.

Despite the positive power of forgiveness, this act is often misunderstood. Let's look a little more closely at what it is and it's not:

Forgiveness is ...

✓ ...a gift to *yourself* that relieves the emotional and physical burdens of resentment

✓ ...a choice to improve your entire life: mentally, physically and spiritually

✓ ...an act performed because you've been wronged (not because the act wasn't wrong)

Forgiveness is not ...

✓ ...forgetting, denying or condoning the event or the pain it caused

✓ ...an act that can only be performed if the other person asks for it, feels remorse or is still in your life: it doesn't rely on anyone but you

✓ ...the same as reconciliation, which needs a resolution between two parties

✓ ...an indication that you will allow the event to happen again

✓ ...a sign of weakness or being a pushover

✓ ...always easy: forgiveness often requires time, energy, strength - and sometimes even assistance

Some people resist forgiveness because they feel the need to punish those who wronged them. In reality, these people end up feeling the most pain.

Others resist forgiving because they believe that what happened was too horrible to ever forgive. These people are also inaccurate: as forgiveness experts agree, no act is too awful to be forgiven.

Consider Dong Yun Yoon, a Korean immigrant whose house was the crash site for a jet that lost control. Dong's wife, two young daughters and mother-in-law were killed in the incident, but Dong himself was at work at the time.

The plane's pilot ejected moments before the impact and survived. About this, Dong pleaded, "Please pray for him not to suffer from this accident... I don't blame him. I don't have any hard feelings. I know he did everything he could."

Forgiving the pilot for this unimaginable tragedy didn't mean that Dong felt no pain for the incident; the new widower fought back tears during a press conference after the event, obviously devastated and heartbroken. "I know there are many people who have experienced more terrible things," he said, "but please tell me how to do it. I don't know what to do."

Coping with a disaster is similar to nursing a deep, cavernous wound. When people don't forgive, however, it's like constantly adding salt to this wound – it prevents the injury from ever fully healing. Forgiveness, of course, won't take away the anguish, but it will stop additional, unnecessary pain from controlling your life.

Your Prescription: Find the strength to forgive

To forgive is the highest, most beautiful form of love. In return, you will receive untold peace and happiness.

**-Robert Muller,
Former Assistant Secretary General
of the United Nations**

If you're finding forgiveness a difficult thing to do, know that you're not alone. For most of us, this act requires changing our mindsets and learning new skills. For example, many of my clients get to the stage where they understand how important forgiveness is, but don't know how to put it into practice. I advise them to do the following:

1. Identify your forgiveness barriers. Obstacles to forgiveness often include:

✓ Unrealistic desires (such as a desire to change the past or have the person who wronged you change)
✓ Not taking accountability for what you *can* do *now*
✓ Viewing yourself as a victim rather than as a champion over challenges

Once you know what these obstacles are, you can begin to overcome them.

2. Identify and accept your reasons for forgiveness. We all have different goals and motivations in our lives. To begin to forgive, we need to know why we want to put energy and effort into doing this. The benefits of forgiveness include:

✓ Improved overall psychological well-being
✓ Enhanced physical health (such as lower blood pressure, heart rate, chronic pain and muscle tension)

- ✓ Improved sleep
- ✓ More energy
- ✓ Healthier and stronger relationships[7]
- ✓ Greater spiritual well-being
- ✓ Lower risk of alcohol/substance abuse
- ✓ Decreased eating of "comfort food"
- ✓ Increased levels of overall happiness

Which of these are most important to you?

3. Find the silver lining. Determine the positives that have come from the experience (people you've met, love you've received, positive changes in your perspective on life etc.) and rewrite the meaning of the event.

Perhaps getting hurt was a learning experience that enabled you to help others, as it was for Susan Lee-Titus? Maybe you've seen how much a friend cares about you from the support she's offered? Whatever the case, don't forget that forgiveness is an empowering, constructive act for you that opens doors to positivity and happiness.

Want more information on how to forgive? Visit www. ahappyyou.com to get free worksheets to help you truly learn the art of forgiveness. The peace and joy that come with forgiving are amazing.

---

7   As Mother Theresa once said, "If we really want to love, we must learn how to forgive."

Name _____

Address _____ Date _____

R℟ FORGIVE YOURSELF AND OTHERS

✓ Release your resentment and reap the benefits

✓ Identify and overcome your barriers to forgiveness

✓ Keep in mind how forgiveness will improve your life

✓ Find the silver lining to situations and focus on positive outcomes (lessons learned, people you met because of the experience etc.)

Signature _____

 G: GOALS

ESTABLISH GOALS TO PRIORITIZE
AND ACHIEVE HAPPINESS

> Goals are like a roadmap: they take you
> wherever you want to go. In doing this, they can
> help you make your dreams come true.

When you hear the word "goals," a parent or school guidance counselor's voice might echo in your head saying, "*You must have goals!*" For some, these can sound more like straightjackets than ways of enhancing happiness.

In reality, the purpose of developing goals is to help us accomplish the things we truly desire in life. Setting goals gives us a roadmap to help us reach our most coveted destinations. When we're working toward the achievements that matter most to us, we're more motivated, have greater energy levels and are happier.

The Diagnosis: Lack of purpose

> *If you want to live a happy life, tie it to a goal,*
> *not to people or things.*
>
> **-Albert Einstein,**
> **Theoretical Physicist**

Which scenario best describes you?

You go through the motions of your day, excited to get home from work (or put the kids to bed) so you can relax and watch TV

OR

You have specific goals (at work and in your personal life) that motivate how you spend your time

If you truly want to be happy, make happiness a priority and work toward accomplishing experiences that will bring you more joy. Stefan Swanepoel is a great example of this:[8]

In 1994 Stefan, his wife and his two sons immigrated to the United States. By the time he was in his early thirties, Stefan had already been schooled and lived in three countries and "wanted to relocate to a place where we could give our children a safer and brighter future (at the time in South Africa, murder, rape and kidnappings were not uncommon) and where I could take my business and writing career to the next level."

When they arrived, however, they knew almost no one and didn't fully understand many aspects of the culture that naturally born citizens take for granted: social security, medical insurance and credit scoring systems, for example. "We had to learn about them all," Stefan recalls.

---

8   For more information on Stefan Swanepoel and real estate trends, visit his website at www.swanepoel.com.

How could they create a happy home in this completely new, uncertain and unknown environment? A successful businessperson who used targets, focus and tenacity to help propel his career in South Africa, Stefan established goals to guide him to happiness and success in the USA. Specifically, he developed long-term goals that helped progress him to where he wanted to be. These included:

Goal to be completed	Goal
3 years	*"Get family settled into the new country" (find a home, job, community etc.)*
7 years	*"Become proud American Citizens"*
10 years	*"Establish myself as THE expert in my chosen field - real estate trends"*
15 years	*"Provide sons quality university education"*

Having these specific milestones helped Stefan remain focused and not become overwhelmed. As a result, he successfully achieved each of these goals within almost the exact time frames planned.

To achieve this, he had to break down his lofty goals into smaller subgoals. Take, for example, his desire to be THE expert in his field. He started at the bottom with no professional reputation in the US, and then took several steps. First, he read and digested everything that had been written on his subject (real estate trends), then looked to see what the current experts were doing - writing books, consulting, speaking etc. - and followed suit.

The next step was to produce something that was more comprehensive than anything available at the time: he decided to write a high quality, one-hundred-sixty page definitive report every twelve months detailing all the business trends impacting the industry nationwide. This had never been done before. Today, after authoring such a report every year for five years, his Swanepoel TRENDS Report has become the gold standard in the real estate industry.

The result of working toward and achieving his goals? A satisfaction with life and a joy that radiates. Spending time with Stefan not only allows you to see the power of goals for achieving your dreams, but also motivates you to want to follow in his goal-setting footsteps.

Your Prescription: Set and achieve goals

Without goals and plans to reach them, you are like a ship that has set sail with no destination.

-Fitzhugh Dodson,
Author and Clinical Psychologist

So, how can you achieve meaningful, life-altering goals like Stefan? Try these five steps:

1. Be proactive and identify your short-term and long-term goals. Don't wait for good things to take place - make them happen. Identify what your ultimate desires are, then break down your long-term goal into short-term aims to prevent you from feeling overwhelmed. This was one of the main keys to Stefan Swanepoel's success.

2. Write down your goals. Your goals are your roadmap to happiness, and you are far more likely to achieve them if you write them down, post them in a visible place and refer to them daily. This keeps them in the forefront of your mind and helps you stay focused on them even in hectic times.

3. Visualize success. Visualizing your achievements is an important aspect of realizing your goals and is a powerful motivator that can help you regain focus if/when you lose your drive.

Close your eyes and imagine that you've just completed your goal. Don't worry about how you did it: just picture yourself having accomplished it. How do you feel? What does success look like? Taste like? Smell like? Are you happy? Imagine yourself in the moment of accomplishment, relishing your victory. Experience all the sensations and really let your body feel what it's going to be like to achieve that target.

4. Learn from obstacles and be flexible. If you're not progressing as well as you'd like to, learn from your setbacks. As Thomas Alva Edison once said about "failed" inventions, "I'm not discouraged, because every wrong attempt discarded is another step forward."

There are times, however, when it's appropriate to modify your goals: circumstances and desires can change. Flexibility, both regarding the goal itself and the means you have in mind for achieving it, is important.

Consider Greg Mortenson, whose story is described in the book Three Cups of Tea. *Greg had a goal to reach the summit of K2, the world's second highest mountain, but bad weather conditions on his planned ascent date prevented this from happening.*

On the way down from his attempt, Greg had a life altering experience. After getting lost and coming close to death, he was cared for by villagers from a small town in Pakistan who he'd never before met. While they were nursing him back to health, he learned about a huge need this village, Korphe, had for a school for girls.

When he recovered, he developed a new goal: to build a school in this remote village. Not only did he achieve this, but he's also gone on to help educate over twenty-five-thousand children across Pakistan.

Why did he do this? Through his experience, he came to view education as the key *solution to terrorism. The result of achieving his revised goal to build schools for children in this area is a fulfilled life for Greg Mortensen and the immeasurable joy experienced by the recipients of his hard work.*

5. Celebrate your successes. Place a checkmark on your calendar when you complete any short-term target. Once you've attained your ultimate goal, reward yourself! Enjoy the satisfaction of hard work realized.

Setting and achieving your goals is an important component of your happiness prescription. As you work towards the accomplishments that are important to you, you'll come to experience increased joy and satisfaction with your life.

Name _____

Address _____ Date _____

Rx ESTABLISH GOALS

✓ Develop a roadmap to happiness by working toward specific goals

✓ Identify short and long-term goals

✓ Write down your goals and review them often

✓ Visualize your success

✓ Learn from obstacles and be flexible

✓ Celebrate your successes

Signature _____

H: HUMOR

GET MORE LAUGHTER AND FUN INTO YOUR LIFE

> *Sometimes I lie awake at night and ask,*
> *"Where have I gone wrong?" Then a voice says to me,*
> *"This is going to take more than one night."*
>
> **-Charles M. Schultz,**
> **Cartoonist**

It goes without saying that humor has a way of making us happier, but did you know that laughter, a common result of humor, has also been proven to be good for your mental and physical health?

Some Benefits of Laughter

Laughter reduces blood pressure levels. When you laugh heartily, your blood pressure briefly increases then decreases. The deep breathing that follows sends oxygen-rich blood and nutrients around your body.

Laughter positively affects your biochemical state. Laughter reduces stress hormones that circulate around our bodies. This results in decreased muscle tension and psychological stress as well as an increase in antibody numbers (which fight infection) and energy levels.

Humor improves brain function. Laughter stimulates learning, enhances creative thinking and can even improve our memories. It also helps us to see events in a different, more positive light.

The Diagnosis: Being too serious

If at first you don't succeed, then skydiving definitely isn't for you.

-Steven Wright,
Comedian

For children, having a good laugh is easy: tickling, a silly story or nonsensical statements are all cause for a giggle. Whenever my young daughters are in a foul mood, I just lighten the atmosphere by pretending that their armpits have gone missing. We then go and search for them or plant new ones together, and whatever was distressing them is quickly forgotten.

Sadly, the stresses and demands of daily life often prevent adults from seeing life's abundant hilarity, which is an important component of happiness.[9] Everyday situations can definitely be funny, as is shown in the following celebrity examples:

- ✓ *Saturday Night Live* star Tina Fey on having to return to work after giving birth to her daughter: "*I had to get back to work . . . NBC has me under contract; the baby and I have only a verbal agreement.*"
- ✓ Dane Cook commenting about an accident: "*He was hit by a Dodge . . . which I found funny and ironic.*"
- ✓ Steve Martin discussing a trip to the doctor: "*First the doctor told me the good news: I was going to have a disease named after me.*"
- ✓ Robin Williams' observation "*If it's the Psychic Network, why do they need a phone number?*"

Both our personal and professional lives can be improved when we introduce positive humor to them. As Sam Walton, the self-made billionaire who founded Wal-Mart and Sam's Club once said, "Celebrate your success and find humor in your failures. Don't take yourself so seriously. Loosen up and everyone around you will loosen up. Have fun and always show enthusiasm. When all else fails, put on a costume and sing a silly song."

Even when times are tough, laughter (or even just a smile) can make the situation seem less bleak. Fill your Humor Rx today and begin seeing the lighter side of life!

Your Prescription: Learn to laugh again

> *Don't sweat the petty things and don't pet the sweaty things.*
>
> **-George Carlin,**
> **Stand-up Comedian and Author**

Here are some simple ways of bringing more humor into your life:

---

9   To improve happiness, the humor must be encouraging and uplifting - not degrading, humiliating or overly cynical.

1. Spend time with funny people. Some people are naturally humorous, and their lightheartedness can be contagious. Spend more time with this kind of person – even actively seeking them out when you need to.

At the same time, also take inventory of the people you currently spend time with and determine if any of them deplete your humor; there are some people who are so negative that they drain positivity from even the most hilarious of events. If you're looking for more happiness and have some humor-sappers in your life, lessen the amount of time you spend with them. Don't feel guilty, either – your health and happiness is at stake here.

2. Poke fun at yourself. Sharing an embarrassing moment with your friends or work associates is an easy way to get a good laugh. While you don't want to be too self-deprecating, pointing out events that highlight your humility can be refreshing. As one comedian said, "I'm not a complete idiot, some parts are missing."

3. Take a lesson from children. Watch kids and observe how easily they play and laugh. Children are great role models for taking life less seriously, and they often do this without even realizing it.

The other day my four-year-old and I were snuggling and reading a book together. She inadvertently touched my calf (which I'd apparently not shaved) and exclaimed, "Mom, your legs are spicy!" Kids really do say the darndest things.

4. Immerse yourself in the comedy genre. Visit a comedy club, read a funny story, watch sitcoms or slapstick movies or sign up to get a "joke of the day" email. With all the bad news that bombards us on TV, the radio and the internet, it's vital to focus on ways to enhance humor and reduce negativity.

The eleven-time Emmy winner Ellen DeGeneres is a witty and personable television show host who uses humor to enhance her own and others' joy. At the 2006 Tulane University graduation, Ellen followed Bill Clinton out on stage wearing a bathrobe and furry slippers. "They told me everyone would be wearing robes," she explained.

Ellen has described an early memory of using humor after her parents got divorced when she was thirteen years old. When her mother was feeling down, "I would start to make fun of her dancing," DeGeneres remembers. "Then she'd start to laugh and I'd make fun of her laughing. Then she'd laugh so hard she'd start to cry, and then I'd make fun of that. I would totally bring her from where I'd seen her start going into depression to all the way out of it." Humor can be very powerful.

At the age of twenty-three, Ellen lost a close friend in a car accident. In an attempt to make sense out of that tragedy, she turned to humor once again. What she created was later part of her routine entitled Conversations with God. *In it, she meets the Creator who, according to Ellen, is a black woman who likes fondue and Chablis wine.*

Ellen's humor is so effective because she uses situations that would not immediately make us laugh otherwise; by looking for the positive, humorous slants on every situation, she makes herself and other people happier.

So, give it a try. Humor can help you to shake off life's stresses and enjoy light-hearted, carefree moments in an otherwise hectic world. Incorporate more humor into your life today and experience increased happiness as a result.

These signs are great examples of humor:

Name _____

Address _____ Date _____

R℞ INCORPORATE MORE HUMOR IN YOUR LIFE

✓ Spend time with amusing people

✓ Have a laugh at your own expense

✓ Take a lesson from the humor experts – children

✓ Immerse yourself in different sources of comedy

Signature _____

1: INSPIRATION

BE INSPIRED TO MAKE THE BEST OF EVERY SITUATION

> Whenever you're in a tough situation, consider how you can "rewrite" it to become an inspiring story. Overcoming challenges in the face of adversity is a great way to boost your self-confidence and happiness levels.

Reading inspirational stories can lift our spirits, help us find the strength to face our own challenges, and make us appreciate our blessings. In short, they have the power to enhance our happiness.

Jack Canfield and Mark Victor Hansen have sold more than one-hundred-and-twelve-million books from their Chicken Soup for the Soul *series by applying this amazing concept and selling inspirational stories.*

The Chicken Soup *authors themselves are an inspirational story, too. After years of writing and compiling their book, they were finally ready to sell their manuscript to a publisher. However, getting the book published proved to be a challenging task. Over the course of three years, more than one-hundred-and-forty publishers rejected their manuscript, with many warning "this won't sell!"*

Despite these rejections, Canfield and Hansen didn't give up. They believed in their book, and when they finally got their stories published, it proved to be the initial step to a multimillion-dollar enterprise.

History also provides many great inspirational stories. Consider just a few:

- ✓ George Washington's father died when he was eleven, so he stopped going to school to help his mother at the plantation. With only seven years of formal schooling, he became one of the greatest leaders this country has ever had.
- ✓ Harriet Tubman escaped unspeakable atrocities as a slave to attain her freedom. Rather than relax in her liberty, however, she then returned to the South almost twenty times to risk her life helping to free more than three-hundred other slaves.
- ✓ Mahatma Gandhi went from being an unknown lawyer to the liberator of India by starting an independence movement that didn't resort to violence. During his quest for freedom, he was beaten, imprisoned four times and faced self-imposed hunger strikes, yet he overcame these obstacles to become one of the world's most inspiring leaders.
- ✓ Lance Armstrong battled cancer and personal crisis. After his diagnosis with testicular cancer, his doctors told him that he wouldn't live, and yet he overcame this grim death sentence to become one of the top (if not *the* top) cyclists in the world, winning the Tour de France a record seven times.

When you read these and other inspiring stories, how do you feel? Positive? Motivated? Energized to do something inspiring yourself?

It's important to remember that inspiring stories don't have to come from famous people, however. We can find inspiration in many everyday situations:

Take Tom Antion, for example. In 1986, Tom was sleeping on a mattress thrown on the floor, unable to afford even a box spring. He was on the verge of losing his rundown apartment and having to live on the street. Tom's business had suffered devastating losses because of new legislation - something out of his control. Rather than wallowing in self-pity, however, he decided he needed a new career.

His motto was: "Being broke is a temporary condition, being poor is a state of mind." In fact, Tom compares himself to the Black Knight character in Monty Python's Holy Grail *who, despite having each of his limbs systematically (and comically) removed by the King Arthur character, continues his determination and perseverance:*

Black Knight: *'Tis but a scratch.*
King Arthur: *A scratch? Your arm's off!*

Tom grew up with little money but plenty of humor and resilience in his household. He used both of these strengths to start a new business: custom-designed practical jokes. He called it "Prank Masters," and taught others to remain upbeat through adversity.

Today Tom is a millionaire several times over. He's also a highly sought-after trainer in the world of internet marketing where he focuses on helping people help others - while also making a profit themselves.[10] He is doing what he truly enjoys doing and is extremely happy (and successful) because of it.

The Diagnosis: Lack of inspiration

Just don't give up on trying to do what you really want to do.
Where there is love and inspiration,
I don't think you can go wrong.

-Ella Fitzgerald,
Jazz Singer

---

10   Thanks to Tom Antion for taking the time to speak with me. For more information on him, visit his website at www.greatinternetmarketingtraining.com.

Ever feel like life is too stressful, too overwhelming and too difficult to find inspirational stories from your personal experiences? In reality, motivating stories usually center on negative events. In fact, they tend to have two main ingredients:

1. A problem that seems overwhelming

2. Overcoming the problem and achieving a meaningful goal

Inspiration comes from seeing or hearing how people's spirits prevail in the face of adversity and hardship.

Consider Eric Lowen of the band Lowen & Navarro. *You may not know the name, but you've probably heard their music:* We Belong, *made popular by Pat Benatar, is one of their biggest hits.*

Eric and his best friend, Dan Navarro, have written songs and performed together for over twenty years. Often spending more than one-hundred nights on the road a year, they've played in clubs, traveled the world and enjoyed the fusion of their passion and profession. Life's been good.

In March 2004, however, Eric was diagnosed with Amyotrophic Lateral Sclerosis (ALS), also known as Lou Gehrig's Disease. ALS is a progressive neurodegenerative condition that affects nerve cells in the brain and the spinal cord - paralyzing different parts of the body until even the diaphragm (responsible for breathing) no longer functions. The average person lives only between three and five years after being diagnosed with the illness.

Despite this fatal prognosis, Eric decided to enjoy living rather than fearing dying. At the time that I write this in 2009, he continues to travel and perform when he can, as well as spending time with his children and other loved ones.

When asked, "How do you do it?" Eric responds, "I just do. What other choice do I have?" In reality, he has many choices, including the option to give up all hope and wait for death to take him. But not

Eric. Seeing him continue to perform, even when his band members have to carry him on stage, is truly inspiring.[11]

Your Prescription: Find your own inspiring voice

If your actions inspire others to dream more, learn more, do more and become more, you are a leader.

**-John Quincy Adams,
6th President of the United States**

Inspiring stories can provide courage and motivation even during difficult times. Try developing an inspirational journal to record stories from your own and others' lives, and then occasionally read over this collection to experience encouragement, motivation and appreciation for the life you lead. In your inspirational journal, include:

1. Stories about your own accomplishments. Think of your proudest triumphs, and remind yourself of the obstacles you overcame and the hardships you endured when achieving these successes. Record your memories of the events - especially how you felt when you realized the accomplishments.

2. Lessons learned in life. Think of particularly challenging and life-altering events in your life - ones that might have triggered spiritual growth or resulted in an important life lesson. What did you learn from them? How did they change you and/or others in a positive way?

Reviewing the lessons you've learned in the past can really inspire you and help you to avoid the same mistakes or pitfalls in the future.

3. Learn inspirational stories from others. In addition to opening

---

11   For more information on Eric Lowen and Dan Navarro, visit their website at www.lownav.com.

yourself to your own life's stories, "tune in" to the stories of others. If you hear a good story about someone, make a note of it in your journal. Over time you'll create a collection of inspiring stories that you can re-read during tough or troublesome periods in your life.

Discover others' inspirational stories by reading (autobiographies or any of the volumes from *Chicken Soup for the Soul* series, for example), listening to inspiring radio interviews (I love Terry Gross's *Fresh Air* on NPR) or watching motivating television shows (such as *Biography* on *A&E*).

Think your life is in too much of a hole to get out of? Think those with inspiring stories didn't have it as bad as you? Consider the list of well-known individuals below. Each one felt so hopeless that they seriously contemplated - or even attempted - suicide before their amazing achievements:

- ✓ Comedian Drew Carey described a difficult childhood that included the death of his father and being molested. He attempted suicide in his late teens, but then went on to live and fulfill his dream of becoming a stand-up comedian and game show host.
- ✓ Author J. K. Rowling revealed that she contemplated suicide, having felt completely hopeless and helpless about her life. Within a few years of this difficult time, however, she was writing her international best-selling *Harry Potter* series.
- ✓ Singer Billy Joel admitted to a suicide attempt in the late 1970s before he received any of his six Grammys or recorded any of his sixteen platinum albums.

Each one of these individuals overcame his or her hopelessness to achieve remarkable feats. Regardless of where you are right now, you can overcome your challenges and become an inspiring story, too.

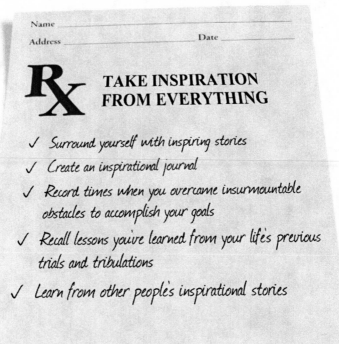

Name _____

Address _____ Date _____

R̶x TAKE INSPIRATION FROM EVERYTHING

✓ Surround yourself with inspiring stories

✓ Create an inspirational journal

✓ Record times when you overcame insurmountable obstacles to accomplish your goals

✓ Recall lessons you've learned from your life's previous trials and tribulations

✓ Learn from other people's inspirational stories

Signature _____

J: JOURNALING

WRITE OUT YOUR EXPERIENCES

> When we move our thoughts from mind to paper, there's a transformation in clarity: negative events can be seen in a different light; positive experiences can be better cherished.

Annelies "Anne" Marie Frank became one of the most famous victims of Nazi persecution during World War II. When Germany invaded the Netherlands, Anne's family hid in a small, secret annex in Amsterdam all crammed together.

For this energetic and extroverted young woman, the attic felt like a prison. To escape, she documented in her journal the political tension of the time and the subsequent impact it had on her personal life. This was therapeutic for the thirteen-year-old, who amazingly was able to see positives even during this most difficult of periods. Anne once wrote, "I don't think of all the misery, but of the beauty that still remains."

Sadly, her life became even worse when, after two years of hiding, Anne and her family were captured by Nazis and put into a concentration camp. Within seven months, Anne was dead.

After her death, Anne's journal was found and returned to her father, Otto. Touched by his daughter's depth of emotion and maturity of writing, he had the document published as a fulfillment of Anne's dream of becoming an author. As a result, her heart-wrenching and heart-warming diary has exposed millions of readers to the terrors of the Holocaust and become one of the most influential pieces of writing of the twentieth century. During such a horrific time, Anne's journal symbolized hope for humanity.

Journaling is the act of writing what's on your mind, charting your experiences and documenting your responses. Keeping a journal can help you concentrate on the positive aspects of your life, come to terms with past events and track your success toward achieving desired goals. Writing out experiences can be an extremely helpful way to lessen stress and enhance happiness.

The Diagnosis: No self-reflection

Journal writing is a voyage to the interior.

- Christina Baldwin,
Master Storyteller

While the thought of journaling may conjure up images of more "pimply" times where writing started with "Dear Diary," it can be a very therapeutic experience on the path to finding happiness.

There are three different types of journaling, all of which can enhance your daily joy:

✓ Positive event
✓ Specific negative event
✓ Tracking your progress

Positive event:

Many of us tend to concentrate on negative events in our everyday lives; we pay attention to what's wrong and filter out positive experiences which are occurring at the same time.

Positive event journaling can abruptly shift the focus of negative thoughts, as writing about the good things in our lives helps us to better identify and appreciate beneficial experiences. If you're consciously scanning your life for something happy to write about, you're more likely to find the good things which happen in your day.

Specific negative events:

Negative events refer to incidents that cause distress, and specific negative event journaling looks at specific negative experiences. While writing about these may initially seem counterintuitive to increasing happiness, it's been shown to positively decrease your stress levels – so long as you do more than just list the events (which may have the opposite effect).

Dr. James Pennebaker has dedicated a good portion of his career to studying the effects of journaling. In one of his experiments, two groups of college students wrote in a journal for twenty minutes each day for three days. The first group was asked to write about trivial tidbits from their lives, while the second was asked to write about the worst trauma that they'd ever experienced. That was all they did.

These students were then followed for the entire semester, and the results were amazing. The first group, which had written about trivial issues, experienced no change to their physical or mental health. In contrast, the second group showed many improvements - including fewer visits to the doctor over the course of the semester, a strengthened immune system and increased psychological well-being.

Research has revealed that writing about a specific traumatic event also:

✓ Helps clarify your thoughts
✓ Aids finding a solution to problems surrounding that event
✓ Assists with forgiveness
✓ Decreases depression and anxiety in the long term
✓ Enhances positive moods

Tracking your progress:

Tracking your progress journaling entails recording behaviors you want to change. This allows you to track your progression while working toward a goal.

For example, if your goal is to lose thirty pounds in eight months, develop a journal that documents your exercise and nutritional intake. This creates motivation *and* accountability for your desired outcome.

Your Prescription: Writing to change your life

> *I never travel without my diary.*
> *One should always have something*
> *sensational to read in the train.*
>
> **-Oscar Wilde,**
> **Poet, Novelist and Critic**

Although journaling involves writing about your thoughts, emotions and experiences, maintaining a journal is far from a chore: it can be a positive, affirming experience that relieves stress and generates greater happiness.

Try the following recommendations:

1. Choose what type of journaling best suits you.
✓ If your goal is to experience stronger gratitude in life, journaling about **positive events** may be your best option. Every day, write down at least three positive events that took place. This simple exercise can drastically improve your attitudes; as we saw in *Chapter*

A: Appreciation, writing about the good things in our lives helps us to better identify and appreciate happy times.

✓ If you're struggling with something that happened in the past that is hindering your happiness, start journaling about that **specific negative event.** Just describe what happened and your reaction to it by writing continuously for about twenty minutes without judgment of content or writing style.

✓ If you're determined to achieve a particular goal that requires hard work, time and perseverance, keeping a journal to **track your progress** can be an amazing motivational and accountability tool. For more information on this topic, see *Chapter G: Goals.*

2. Just do it - write away. Spelling and grammar aren't important: this isn't an assignment in English class, so just write freely without worries.

3. Read what you write.

✓ When recording positive events, read over your journal every day. Again, the more positives you're aware of, the more you'll notice the effects of a new outlook in the future. Positivity is self-reproducing.

✓ If you're recording a specific, difficult experience, assess how accurate and useful your interpretation of the event is. If it helps, take assistance from the tools in this book or from someone you trust.

✓ For those whose journals focus on logging steps towards a specific goal, read over your progress. Are you staying on track? Reward yourself and be proud. Not exactly where you want to be? Explore why that is and make any necessary changes.

4. Remember that you don't have to share your journal. Some of my clients who journal about specific negative events destroy what they write once they've "got it out" and reflected on it. This makes sure no one else reads their inner-most thoughts. Other people prefer to share their journals very publically through blogs etc. that both friends and strangers can access. The privacy level of your journal is totally up to you.

Anne Frank's diary gave her a place to find personal peace in the most trying of times, and journaling can do the same for you: get started today and see how your happiness and serenity levels improve.

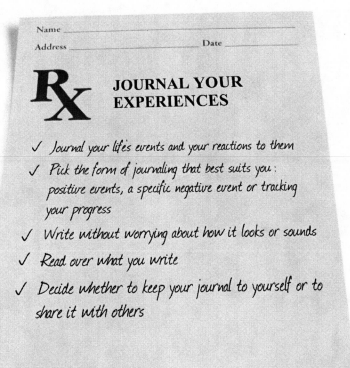

Name _____

Address _____ Date _____

℞ JOURNAL YOUR EXPERIENCES

✓ Journal your life's events and your reactions to them

✓ Pick the form of journaling that best suits you: positive events, a specific negative event or tracking your progress

✓ Write without worrying about how it looks or sounds

✓ Read over what you write

✓ Decide whether to keep your journal to yourself or to share it with others

Signature _____

K: KINDNESS

BE KIND TO OTHERS AND REAP THE BENEFITS YOURSELF

Never underestimate the power of kind acts: the more you give to others, the more emotional and spiritual gifts you receive for yourself.

Leigh Ann and Sean Tuohy were driving by their daughter's school one cold November afternoon when they saw a young man walking in the snow wearing nothing but shorts and a t-shirt. They turned the car around and asked this teen if he needed any help. As Michael Oher got into the car, his life and the Tuohys' changed forever.

Michael had been born as one of thirteen children to a crack-addicted mother and an absent father who was later murdered. In and out of foster homes, he attended eleven different schools during his first nine years as a student. There were many times when "home" to him meant a mattress on someone's porch and begging for food.

When he was sixteen, Michael was temporarily staying with someone who recommended he attend a Christian school. It was here that the Tuohys and Michael met. The family invited him to stay with them.

As Sean put it, we "looked into his heart and saw that he needed more than just food." Leigh Ann described, "Michael just needed to be loved. I hugged him for a year before he ever hugged me back.

And I think that was the first time in his life that he really in his heart knew that someone loved him for him."

The stay at the Tuohy's eventually evolved into an official adoption; Michael went from being alone to being a loved family member - all because of the kind hearts of the Tuohy family.

That, in and of itself, is an incredible account of how compassion can transform lives. But the story continues.

After not playing football for two years because of his previously unstable personal life, Michael started playing again as a junior when he was sixteen. Within months, he became one of the most highly recruited high school players. The following year he received numerous scholarship offers from top-ranked schools. He eventually chose to attend the University of Mississippi, his adopted parents' alma mater, where he continued his success on the field.

In the NFL 2009 draft, Michael Oher was drafted in the first round by the Baltimore Ravens – a dream come true for any boy who's ever played football, and a dream made possible by the kindness of Leigh Ann and Sean Tuohy.

You don't have to adopt a child to make a difference in the lives of others. Even offering almost effortless gestures (such as a simple smile) can go a long way.

When you help someone, you not only help the individual receiving the aid, but also yourself; performing kind acts for others is one of the most satisfying and gratifying things you can do with your time. Like so many other components of your happiness prescription, it doesn't even have to cost you a dime.

Performing kind acts such as volunteering has been shown to help you:

✓ Boost self-confidence
✓ Decrease stress
✓ Learn new skills
✓ Explore a hobby or interest
✓ Make new friends

- ✓ Apply your values to real-life situations
- ✓ Experience a sense of purpose to your life
- ✓ See life in a different, more helpful light (less "sweating of the small things")
- ✓ Enjoy better physical health and live a longer life!

The Diagnosis: A need for more kind acts

> *We make a living by what we get, but we make a life by what we give.*
>
> **-Winston Churchill,**
> **Former Prime Minister of the United Kingdom**

In my clinical practice, I encourage the majority of my clients to volunteer. Why? Volunteering is like free therapy.

Take my former client, Stephanie, as an example. When we first started working together, she was suffering from chronic pain, depression, poor self-esteem and loneliness. Stephanie's whole world was centered on her emotional and physical pain. Her days were spent going to various doctors' offices or lying in bed consumed with her misery.

During therapy, Stephanie told me about a dog she had as a child - an animal she loved dearly. Given her functional state at the time, having a pet of her own wasn't a viable option - but volunteering with dogs was.

After a few minutes of internet research, Stephanie found a nearby dog rescue shelter which didn't euthanize its inhabitants. Two days each week, she went to the shelter to play with the dogs. She spent about fifteen minutes of one-on-one time with them, giving these homeless pooches the attention they so desperately craved. Sometimes she stayed for hours - not because she had to, but because she wanted to and could.

During her time at the shelter, she saw a huge transformation in the dogs. They started eating better, had more energy and seemed to smile whenever they saw her. The best part, though, was that Stephanie went through a similar transformation: her pain became more manageable; her depression decreased and self-confidence grew; she felt a sense of purpose; she loved her time with the dogs and the other volunteers.

. When you help others, your focus often shifts from what you don't have in your life to what you *do* have, and from your stresses to the positives you're contributing to others. Acts of compassion toward other people enhance your own happiness.

Your Prescription: Give the gift of unconditional kindness

> *Kindness is the language which the deaf can hear and the blind can see.*
>
> **-Mark Twain,**
> **Author and Humorist**

Unconditional acts of kindness help enhance happiness in both the receiver and the giver. In our busy world, it's also good to know that kind acts don't need to be complicated, time-consuming or expensive to be effective. Here are some examples of how to simply incorporate compassion into your life:

1. Do at least one nice thing for someone every day. Kind acts can be anything from a warm greeting to volunteering, and you can do them at any point during your daily routine without expending a significant amount of time or financial contribution. Try one of these suggestions today:

- ✓ Send a thank you card to someone for anything they've done (even being a good friend)
- ✓ Hold open a door for someone
- ✓ Smile . . . at anyone
- ✓ Compliment your spouse, a friend or a co-worker

✓ Thank people who assist you, even if doing so is their "job" (a cashier, your mother etc.)

✓ Give a good tip to your food server even if the meal wasn't great (don't shoot the messenger if the cook wasn't the best)

✓ Listen to others

2. Personalize your volunteer work. You can take your kind acts a step further by volunteering your time to a worthy cause. There are countless volunteering opportunities out there. What's important is to find an activity that you'll enjoy and that will be truly meaningful to you. To find the best opportunity, consider the following questions:

✓ Do you want to help locally or in another community?

✓ Do you want to volunteer on a consistent basis (e.g. two hours every week) or as needed (e.g. helping at a one-time fundraiser)?

✓ Do you want to work with other people or would you prefer quiet alone time (such as stuffing envelopes while catching up on your favorite TV program)?

✓ Who or what are you most passionate about? Children? The elderly? Animals? Physically ill individuals? The environment?

✓ What do you enjoy doing? Cooking? Speaking with others? Being physically active? Find something you like so you are excited to do it.

Identify what you most want to do, then find the organization that best fits your interests and get involved. If a specific opportunity doesn't come to mind, try Googling some general ideas or visit a volunteer website like www.volunteermatch.org.

No matter what you do, remember that the good you're putting out into the world will be returned to you. As former

First Lady Nancy Reagan once said, "I'm a big believer that eventually everything comes back to you. You get back what you give out." Doing good deeds for others will make you feel happier and more self-confident, and will also increase your satisfaction with life in general.

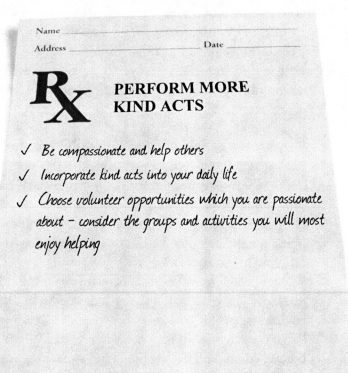

Name
Address _____ Date _____

R̵x PERFORM MORE KIND ACTS

✓ Be compassionate and help others
✓ Incorporate kind acts into your daily life
✓ Choose volunteer opportunities which you are passionate about – consider the groups and activities you will most enjoy helping

Signature _____

L: LOVE

LOVE YOUR FRIENDS AND FAMILY

> Love your friends and family as if it's their last day
> on earth: you never know when it really will be.

In 1980, Nancy Goodman Brinker's only sister "Suzy" died at the young age of thirty-six from breast cancer. Before her death, Suzy frequently expressed a desire to make the entire cancer experience better for other women. Out of love and compassion for others, she asked Nancy to promise to do something to help the millions of women who would be diagnosed with breast cancer at some point in their lives. Out of her love for her sister as well as the other affected women she didn't know, Nancy agreed to do what she could.

Almost thirty years later, Susan G. Komen For The Cure *has given more than $1 billion to help stop breast cancer and support those affected by it. It's Nancy's devotion and concern for others that started this incredible organization, and it's the intense love of thousands of employees and volunteers that keeps* Komen *going.*

If you've ever been to a Komen *event such as the* Race for the Cure®*, you'll know that the love there is practically palpable. It seems like everyone is hugging everyone else - almost a massive love-in. Seeing someone wearing a pink shirt sends a chill up my spine - not only because it signifies this person is a breast cancer survivor, but also because of the overwhelming love she receives even from complete strangers.*

Sharing love with others is an important step to improving your mental and emotional well-being. Surrounding yourself with loving social support helps to encourage healthy habits, fight disease and depression, reduce stress and maintain a positive outlook on life. In short, being with loved ones is an important way of making your life happier.

The Diagnosis: Insufficient social support

> *Shower the people you love with love*
> *Show them the way you feel*
> *Things are gonna be much better if you only will.*
>
> **-James Taylor,**
> **Grammy Award-Winning Singer-Songwriter**

Do you:

- ✓ Have trouble finding someone you feel comfortable confiding in?
- ✓ Often feel lonely?
- ✓ Feel too busy to spend quality time with friends and family?

If you've answered yes to any of the above questions, you may need to examine your social support network. Close, caring relationships offer opportunities to express and receive love - both of which are important components of a joyful life. Intimate personal relationships can also ward off loneliness and provide support even in difficult times.

Consider Cari Shane Parven. Despite having a great life "on paper" (a supportive husband, two healthy children, a job she enjoyed etc.), she felt like something was missing.

One day, right before her fortieth birthday, Cari stood in her kitchen thinking about how she wanted to celebrate this momentous occasion. She realized that, while she had acquaintances she spent time with, she had no major connections or significant friendships. Despite having a wonderful husband and children, she felt alone: "It was like I had abandoned womankind." She vowed right then and there to do something about it by making a commitment to developing friendships. She reached out to women she liked and prioritized spending time with them.

A dedicated worker, Cari admitted it wasn't always easy: "I would have a bunch of work deadlines coming up and hear the phone ring. I felt like a giant was stepping down on me with all the job responsibilities I had, and it would have been much easier to ignore the calls. But I answered them. I pushed myself to stick with my commitment to friendship." Three years later, the results are wonderful.

Not only has Cari developed some amazingly supportive relationships, but her whole life has also transformed. "I have such a peace and joy I never knew was possible. It's as if my shoulders dropped." She describes greater self-esteem, less stress and a sense of being a better mother, wife and worker because of the harmony she experiences by having female friends in her life. "My friendships give me a level of happiness I didn't even know I was missing." Cari chronicles her experiences in her essay Finding Friendship at Forty.

Your Prescription: Cultivate a loving support network

Shared joy is a double joy; shared sorrow is half a sorrow.
-Swedish Proverb

Having more loving relationships in your life will help enhance your happiness level. Let's look at some ways to blossom your social support:

1. Open yourself up to new relationships. When we were in school it was much easier to make new friends, but as life progresses there seem to be fewer opportunities for meeting people. Here are some ideas for extending your social network:

- ✓ **Enjoy the outdoors.** Walk your dog, play with your kids, enjoy the fresh air or go for a run – whatever you do outside, look for others with similar interests.
- ✓ **Become a volunteer.** Donate your time to a cause you feel passionate about and meet new people who share your interests.
- ✓ **Take classes.** Learn something new and enjoy taking a class at a local university, community center or craft store. You'll meet new people who have similar areas of enthusiasm.
- ✓ **Join a support group.** If you're struggling with something, find a group which meets to address the problem. Look for groups that support a solution (how to make things better) instead of the problem (those wallowing in self-pity).

2. Be a good friend. Having good relationships requires both giving *and* taking; in order to grow strong, lasting friendships, it's important to be a good friend. The following tips can help you develop stronger, more nurturing relationships:

- ✓ **Keep in touch, be empathetic and be appreciative.** Return phone calls and e-mails promptly, and better yet, initiate those correspondences. Take note of meaningful events in your friends' lives (a presentation at work, family coming to visit etc.) and reach out when those occasions come around. Also, express appreciation for the love and support you receive.
- ✓ **Eliminate childish competitions.** Be happy when your friends succeed. Comparisons and jealousy won't just

turn off your friends - they'll also make you feel worse about yourself. Celebrate accomplishments with them and they'll share in your joys, too.

✓ **Let it go.** Almost everyone has a loved one who's wronged them in some way, and if you're human you have most likely done something wrong to someone you love at least once, too. It's all part of life. While you can't change the past, you can change the present and future. Forgive your friends and family to bring more happiness into your life and theirs. If you need help with this, refer to *Chapter F: Forgiveness.*

3. Make sure your social network supports you. The purpose of a loving social support network is to increase your happiness and minimize your stress levels – not to send your anxiety levels through the roof or to overwhelm you with obligations. Watch for these clues of unhealthy relationships as you evaluate your friendships:

✓ **Be careful of codependent relationships.** Making friends with people who are struggling to overcome the same unhealthy habits as you can *sometimes* be damaging to your well-being. For example, if a friend encourages you to continue harmful behaviors, end the relationship: it'll be healthier for both of you.

✓ **Don't be a slave to your sense of duty.** If a buddy's consistently demanding repayment for her efforts, you may be better off without her.

✓ **Choose the right support for the situation.** It's impossible for one person to meet 100% of your emotional needs - we all have different strengths. Choose the right support for what you need. For example, if you want to go see a "chick flick," your girlfriend might be a better option than your male mate.

Surrounding yourself with loved ones is essential to finding happiness in life. Prioritize developing strong, trusting relationships and working to maintain them. You'll soon feel more peace and joy as you share life's ups and downs with those you care about.

Name _____

Address _____ Date _____

℞ LOVE YOUR FAMILY AND FRIENDS

✓ Prioritize spending quality time with loved ones
✓ Make new friends (volunteer, take classes, join a group etc.)
✓ Be a good friend (be empathetic, appreciative and forgiving)
✓ Make sure your social network supports you

Signature _____

M: MINDFULNESS

ENJOY WHAT'S HAPPENING RIGHT NOW

> The past and future are important, but don't miss
> out on the present: it will soon be gone!

In our fast-paced society, we often obsess about the future or get consumed with the past. While periodically reflecting on what will happen and what has happened already certainly aren't bad things, dwelling on and worrying about them doesn't promote happiness. We often forget the value of being in the moment and enjoying life as events unfold around us. This sort of unhealthy focus is something I frequently see in my practice.

Lisa was a worrywart. "I always have been," she told me during our first session together. "I worry about anything there is to worry about: what my boyfriend means when he's 'coming over to see me'; if my boss' reaction to a situation means she's going to fire me; whether my electronic payment will get to the credit card company on time, even though the bank's website says it will."

Lisa also stressed that what she had said or done in the past offended someone. "I constantly play over what happened in my mind and then get upset at myself for stupid comments or klutzy moves. I just beat myself up."

Her worry did not stay in the past because Lisa fretted over the future, too. "What if I lose my job in this bad economy? I mean, how will I ever get another job? And I really only have enough savings for three months of bills. Then I will have to dip into my retirement. So I will never be able to retire. And if I spend all that, I will have to live on the street…"

Worrying about the past and future were crippling her with stress. She was so overwhelmed by regret of what she "should have done" and anxious about what might be that she was missing out on her life.

When she came to me for help with the situation, I asked her to imagine speaking to herself in five years if, in fact, she did lose her home and all her savings. "What advice would that future Lisa give the present Lisa?" I asked. Without hesitation, she blurted out, "Enjoy what you have right now!"

It was as if a light bulb went off in her head. By realizing her worry was preventing her from enjoying what she had right then, she started to see the importance of being more mindful of the here and now.

During therapy, I helped Lisa get rid of her worries about the past and future. The improvements in her life were remarkable. Her stress levels decreased and her happiness skyrocketed. She received a promotion at work ("I stopped worrying and just did my work; it was amazing how much I was able to accomplish"). Even her relationship with her boyfriend benefited. "Because I'm not worrying so much about work, I stopped constantly checking my Blackberry. Now I can relax and really enjoy being with him."

Lisa is a wonderful example of someone who discovered **mindfulness**: being in the present moment. When we're mindful, we're aware of thoughts and sensations that are occurring right now *without passing any judgment* on what's going on.

Research demonstrates that there are multiple benefits to mindfulness, including:

✓ Less stress
✓ Reduced depression and anxiety

- ✓ Improved concentration and creativity
- ✓ Enriched relationships
- ✓ Being better able to cope with difficult situations
- ✓ Enhanced immune function
- ✓ Less muscular tension and pain
- ✓ Greater appreciation of life

The Diagnosis: Faulty focus

Pick the day. Enjoy it to the hilt... The past, I think, has helped me appreciate the present, and I don't want to spoil any of it by fretting about the future.

-Audrey Hepburn,
Actress and Humanitarian

Remembering the past and planning for the future are certainly important. These trains of thought only become problems when they're sources of significant stress to you. For example, how much time do you spend dwelling on the past with regret? Do you, like Lisa, replay events over and over in your mind, thinking "if only this had happened" or "I should have done that"?

Maybe you "live" in the past because you see those times as happier: you were young, in love, in a "better place"? Appreciating the past can certainly be positive, but if you hold the belief that the past is "as good as it gets," this can become a self-fulfilling prophecy.

In contrast, maybe you're not one who lives in the past so much as the one who worries about the future? How often do you stress out about what you *think* will (or won't) happen? How motivating and encouraging are these thoughts?

There's a saying that 97% of what you worry about never happens. I'd go a bit further: even when something you worry about *does* happen, the chances are good that worrying about it won't help you. That's not to say that planning for the future is bad, as it's extremely important – but emotionally reacting as if something horrible is already occurring can cripple you with fear.

Focusing *solely* on the past or future prevents you from enjoying your life. Both are potential roadblocks to true happiness.

Your Prescription: Live in the present

The most precious gift we can offer others is our presence. When mindfulness embraces those we love, they will bloom like flowers.

**-Thich Nhat Hanh,
Vietnamese Monk and Activist**

If you're like most people (myself included), you could probably use some tips on how to improve your mindfulness. Try the following suggestions and notice how being more mindful boosts your happiness:

1. Practice being in the moment and stop multi-tasking. Stop and smell the roses: focus on one activity at a time rather than multi-tasking (truth be told, this is an especially challenging mission for me). Recruit all of your senses to really experience your current state.

As an example, try this exercise for mindful eating by sitting down with a small food such as a grape. Get rid of any distractions (turn off the TV, radio and your cell phone etc.), and then pay full attention to the grape using each of your different senses:

Sight: Look at its color and shape
Touch: Notice what it feels like in your fingers and your mouth: the texture, temperature and weight
Smell: What does it smell like?
Taste: How does it taste: the skin, the juice?
Sound: What does it sound like when you take a bite?
Thoughts: What's going through your mind right now?
Feelings: How are you feeling at the moment?

Who knew eating a single grape could be so sensuous?

This exercise can help enhance mindfulness in general. It's also an exercise I use when working with clients who want to lose weight, as mindful eating can be an important part of achieving and maintaining a healthy figure. Rather than wolfing down a bag full of chips, try eating mindfully. Enjoy each bite. You'll probably eat a lot less and appreciate what you do eat much more.

2. Experience your feelings. Experiencing your emotions is vital, and mindfulness is a great tool for doing this. Stop and ask yourself: "What emotions am I having right now?" and determine what physical sensations you feel, too. Don't pass judgment or try to minimize them – just acknowledge and experience the feelings you have.

Feelings are often heightened by judgments and interpretations we make. Examples include:

- ✓ Fortune-telling (*"This is never going to get better"*)
- ✓ Helplessness (*"There's nothing I can do"*)
- ✓ Regret (*"I should've done things differently"*)
- ✓ Extreme thinking (*"Now I'll never work again"*)

When you allow yourself to notice and experience your feelings without passing judgment, their intensity often *decreases* while your sense of empowerment *increases*.

3. Remember that you're more than just your thoughts, emotions, physical sensations and actions. These are a *part* of who you are, but because these things are not you, you can "step back" and observe them in a detached manner. You might astonish yourself with the things that you think, feel, say and do as you try this.

4. Practice patience. This is definitely not an easy one for me. Before I became a mother, my free time was spent doing dozens of items on my to-do list, and when I encountered an inefficient individual who delayed my productivity . . . well, let's just say I might not have been the most tolerant of people.

Having children changed me, and now helps me (translation: forces me) to practice my patience and mindfulness. When we're racing to get out of the house and my two-year-old refuses to take any assistance in putting on her shoes, I try to take a step back and truly appreciate this tiny, independent being. Her concentration and her attempts at determining which shoe goes on which foot and which way they go on . . . it's truly an amazing sight that I'd miss if I insisted on throwing those shoes on myself (of course, sometimes that *is* necessary!).

Begin taking the time to live in the moment and experience all that life has to offer. Your happiness will increase as you practice and get better at bringing greater mindfulness into your day-to-day existence.

Name _____

Address _____ Date _____

℞ ENJOY WHAT'S HAPPENING RIGHT NOW

✓ Practice being mindful

✓ Stop multi-tasking

✓ Pay attention to and appreciate what's going on in the moment

✓ Identify your feelings without passing judgment

✓ Remember – you're more than your thoughts, emotions, physical sensations and actions

✓ Practice patience

Signature _____

N: NUTRITION

EAT YOUR WAY TO HAPPINESS[12]

> What you put in your mouth affects your psychological
> health as much as it does your physical health.

We've all heard the saying "you are what you eat," but how
does this relate to happiness? What we eat affects our minds and
bodies, and this goes far beyond the concept that living on greasy
food makes you fat.

As an example, have you ever eaten a bagel for breakfast only
to be hungry, tired and maybe even a little irritable a few hours
later? This might be because of a depletion (after an initial spike)
in blood sugar caused by the consumption of white grains and
sugars. What we ingest (or fail to ingest) can significantly affect
our moods.

---

12   This chapter was written with the assistance of Sandra Keros at
www.sandrakeros.com.

The Diagnosis: Poor eating habits

> *He that takes medicine and neglects diet*
> *wastes the skill of the physician.*
>
> **- Chinese Proverb**

At thirty-one, Sandra Keros and her husband embarked on an exciting new adventure: a move across the country. It turned out to be an adventure that changed her life, and one which taught her a lesson she would never forget: the importance of clean, healthy, whole foods.

One morning, this active young woman and avid runner awoke in excruciating pain. Her hips felt like they were on fire; she couldn't walk, stand or even sit without debilitating pain. For four years she consulted with countless specialists, medical doctors, surgeons, chiropractors, acupuncturists and massage therapists until, desperate to find a solution, she reached out to a nutritionist friend who suspected a food allergy to be the cause of the issue. This information, combined with a chiropractor's opinion that a hormonal imbalance was the problem, led her to a turning point.

Determined to get back on the road to recovery, she worked with a holistically-trained doctor who tailored a plan to help her heal. She explains that she was diagnosed with multiple food sensitivities, hormonal imbalance, thyroid disease, fibromyalgia and dangerously high heavy metal levels. "I was shocked to find out that toxins in water, air, everyday products and certain foods – especially because of the way they were processed - were the root cause of all these ailments," she recalled.

Within six months of returning to home cooking, detoxing her home and switching to more natural products, Sandra "felt like a brand new woman. I even shed fifteen pounds without trying and kept it off. What was truly extraordinary, however, was the realization that, when I was living and eating cleanly, my whole attitude to life changed – it was like a fog had been lifted from my eyes, letting me finally think and see clearly."

Today, her passion for food extends into selecting only the best farm-fresh ingredients for her meals: it gives her creative joy and freedom that she enthusiastically shares with her friends and family. She also records her discoveries and health-related thoughts in her blog and enjoys helping others through her nutritional knowledge and creative food passion in a variety of ways – including public speaking, media interviews and her Cooking with Confidence *series.*

Why is our nation's addiction to junk food so detrimental? Though inexpensive and readily available, fast food can be loaded with "bad" fats, chemicals and other unnatural fillers. In addition to hindering our physical health, junk food may also play havoc on our mental health - including our happiness. In fact, for some, diet can even affect the onset, severity and duration of depression.

The problem isn't just fast food hamburgers and supersized fries, though: excessive consumption of caffeine (found in tea, coffee, soda or chocolate) interferes with mineral absorption, can trigger the onset of depression and can even overstimulate the central nervous system to cause mood swings and hypersensitivity. How easy is it to be happy under these conditions?

By eating foods that enhance your happiness, your nutritional intake can be a vital component of your happiness prescription.

Your Prescription: Eat the right foods

> *It's difficult to think anything but pleasant thoughts while eating a homegrown tomato.*
>
> **-Lewis Gizzard,**
> **Writer and Humorist**

The top reasons for eating fast food are its consistency, convenience and cost: we know what we're getting, we don't have to worry about making it and it's relatively cheap.

Interestingly, though, eating well can be the same, too. Take the Emmy award-winning chef Rachael Ray as an example:

As an enthusiastic and sometimes goofy cook, Rachael Ray found her own personal happiness in the kitchen: she now teaches millions of busy individuals (via her TV shows, books and magazine) how to fit healthy meals into their hectic lifestyles.

With Sicilian grandparents and parents who owned several restaurants, Rachael grew up eating Italian food nearly every night. By the time she was four, she'd already discovered her love of food. One of her earliest memories is of watching in awe as her mother cooked: "She was flipping something with a spatula. I tried to copy her and ended up grilling my right thumb!"

In her early twenties, Rachael was ready to take on bigger challenges and so moved to New York City where she lived "paycheck to paycheck" before landing a job at Macy's candy counter. It was here that she first learned to work with gourmet foods. She eventually came to manage a gourmet marketplace, but was soon ready to take on new challenges.

Her popularity exploded when she accepted a position as a chef at a market in Albany, New York where she began thirty-minute cooking classes to teach people that cooking didn't have to be difficult, dreaded or time-consuming. These helped to launch her television career, and it wasn't long before she'd landed a spot on the Food Network *and her life was changed forever.*

Rachael's passion and positive attitude are contagious: "I was raised in a household that taught us that everybody has the right to have a lot of fun." By combining this wisdom and her love for food, she found a personal contentment that radiates through to her audience.

How can you enjoy better nutrition and its many benefits? Consider the following recommendations:

1. Eat periodically throughout the day. Have you ever noticed how you feel when you're hungry? Not eating for extended periods can adversely affect your mood, your ability to concentrate and how productive you are. To optimize your mood and energy, try eating three moderately sized meals and two snacks throughout the day.

2. Ditch the junk and find healthy alternatives. Try to avoid eating too many processed items like chips and candy that don't really satisfy; harmful chemicals in some junk foods can cause your body to struggle, which may be a significant reason why our energy levels and moods fluctuate when we eat them. Instead, focus on "handy" nutritious snacks like in-season fruit (apples, oranges, grapes, etc.), whole-grain crackers, pretzels, dried fruit (raisins, cranberries) and nuts.

Another great snack is called the "happy berry." Th e goji berry, also called the wolfberry, has been touted for centuries as improving physical and psychological health. In fact, a double blind study found that people who consumed GoChi (the brand name of a gogi berry juice) reported increased energy levels, athletic performance, quality of sleep, ease of awakening, ability to focus on activities, mental agility, calmness and general feelings of health and contentment when compared to the placebo group.

3. Make your own food. The food we make at home is often healthier and fresher than the food we buy in restaurants. Don't worry, though - you don't have to go total gourmet or even have a lot of free time to do this well! Buy a good crock-pot and let your food cook throughout the day, or try cooking large batches of your favorite foods on the weekends and storing them in smaller containers for meals during the week.

Not sure how to cook? Try cooking classes. Even better: take one with a friend.

4. Don't go low-fat/nonfat. When I was in college, I had the amazing experience of spending a semester studying in France and living with a French family. I distinctly remember how one day, my French "sister" expressed her opinion that high obesity rates in the US were due to the nonfat diet fad that was all the craze at the time. I thought "*Es-tu dingue?* (Are you crazy?)," but it turns out there might have been some truth to what she said.

Getting the right kind of fat is an important component of a healthy diet. In fact, studies show that diets characterized by consuming low levels of or no fat can make moods worse. When combined with exercise and a nutritious diet, a moderate amount of fat can do wonders for how you feel. Try to consume good, clean sources of animal (such as free-range chicken) and vegetable fat (like avocados) in appropriate amounts to get the balance.

5. Figure out what works for you. Everyone has a body that's unique, and every body will react to foods in different ways (those of you with food allergies already know this). As a result, you need to pay attention to *your* body and tailor your diet to its individual needs.

Start your day well with a breakfast that's right for your metabolic type. For example: some people can go for hours on a breakfast of eggs and vegetables, while others have more energy with fruit and grains. Experiment and find what's right for you.

Sandra Keros recommends you get tested for allergies, as well; many people have low-grade "latent" allergies to fish, dairy, gluten, corn, soy and a number of other foods. If these go undetected, you might inadvertently be worsening your health and mood when you eat them![13]

Eat well and be happier for it; enjoy what you eat, and eat to enjoy your life.

---

13   For more information on testing for food allergies, go to www.sandrakeros.com/BlogRetrieve.aspx?BlogID=2028&PostID=45340.

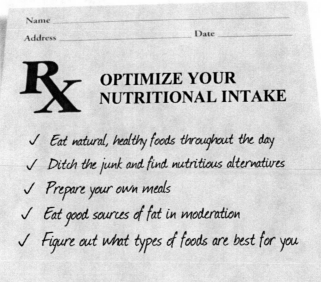

Name _____

Address _____ Date _____

℞ OPTIMIZE YOUR NUTRITIONAL INTAKE

✓ Eat natural, healthy foods throughout the day

✓ Ditch the junk and find nutritious alternatives

✓ Prepare your own meals

✓ Eat good sources of fat in moderation

✓ Figure out what types of foods are best for you

Signature _____

O: OPTIMISM

BE OPTIMISTIC AND REALISTIC

> A glass with half its water is half-full AND half-empty.
> Both are accurate, so it's up to you how you see it.

Seeing everything that happens in a positive light might sound like a good idea, but can it make you miss what's really going on? There's a common perception that pessimists only see the bad in the world while optimists ignore everything that isn't good. In reality, however, this isn't accurate.

True optimists are aware of life's negative aspects, but they only see them as "bumps in the road": they might affect how comfortable a journey feels to make, but they won't stop it from being a generally positive experience. Real optimism is far from a "Pollyanna" world-view that blindly denies the existence of the negative – instead, it acknowledges problems and addresses them face-on. Optimists see the glass as half-full, but *realistically* half-full.

In addition to more hopefulness, these people also enjoy a host of additional benefits when compared with pessimists:

Optimists tend to . . .

- ✓ enjoy greater physical health
- ✓ experience less depression and anxiety
- ✓ exhibit greater resilience
- ✓ appreciate greater successes
- ✓ be more creative at solving problems effectively
- ✓ enjoy a greater quantity and quality of friendships
- ✓ lead more active and fulfilling lives
- ✓ perform better in sports
- ✓ be happier!

Pessimists tend to...

- ✓ suffer from poorer physical health
- ✓ have higher rates of infectious disease
- ✓ be at risk of earlier mortality
- ✓ experience more anxiety, depression, post-traumatic stress disorder and general stress
- ✓ have more strained work and personal relationships
- ✓ be less happy!

As a great example of optimism, let's look at a Hall of Famer:

In 1991, basketball phenomenon Earvin "Magic" Johnson received startling news: blood taken during a routine physical exam showed him to have the Human Immunodeficiency Virus (HIV) which causes AIDS. "Everyone thought I was going to die like a year later," Johnson said.

While others might have seen this diagnosis as a death sentence and just waited for their lives to finish, Magic's classic determination and optimism flourished.

Almost twenty years later, he's still very healthy. "I'm following my doctor's program and I'm making sure I get exercise and a proper diet," he says. "It's been mind over matter, too. I always felt I was going to beat HIV. I had to put that in my mind and live and breathe that every day."

This isn't to say that people who die from AIDS can prevent their deaths by being optimistic, of course, but it does show how optimism can inspire positive behavior such as taking care of yourself even in the most difficult of circumstances.

Optimism also motivates people to help out others; Magic and his foundations have donated almost $10 million to HIV/AIDS organizations and thousands of hours to educating the public and policymakers about HIV.

Using the same optimism and resilience seen on the basketball court when he propelled his team to come from behind to win, Magic has made, and continues to make, the most of his unfortunate diagnosis. We can learn a lot from his optimism and the happiness he experiences despite his affliction.

The Diagnosis: Pessimistic lenses

A pessimist sees the difficulty in every opportunity; an optimist sees the opportunity in every difficulty.

**-Winston Churchill,
Former Prime Minister of the United Kingdom**

In general, what do you think your mindset is? Where do you fall on the scale of optimism to pessimism? Take this brief quiz to determine your level of realistic optimism:

1. When bad things happen in your life, who do you blame?
   A. You.
   B. Unfortunate circumstances.

2. When something good happens, what are you most likely to think?
   A. Wow, I'm so lucky!
   B. Yeah! My hard work's paid off!

3. You get into a fender bender. What's your reaction?
    A. Th ings like this always happen to me.
    B. I'll be more careful next time.

4. An old friend calls you from out of the blue to ask a favor. Which are you more likely to think?
    A. People always use me.
    B. She knows I can help her.

5. Your boss asks you to help with a big project. What's most likely to go through your mind?
    A. Once again, I'm getting dumped on.
    B. Th is will be a great opportunity to get some face time with the higher-ups.

Now, add up all of your As and Bs; A answers correspond to a more pessimistic view point, and B answers represent greater realistic optimism.

Which one was stronger for you? If you got mostly As, study the next section carefully to find ways to increase your level of realistic optimism. Your physical and emotional health will thank you for it.

If you scored mostly Bs, you're already benefiting from your thinking. Read on to learn how to continue to think and live more optimistically.

Your Prescription: Learn to see the glass as realistically half-full

> *When one door closes another door opens,*
> *but we so often look so long and so regretfully*
> *upon the closed door that we do not see*
> *the ones which open for us.*

-Alexander Graham Bell,
Inventor and Perpetual Optimist

How can you enjoy more realistic optimism in your life? Try the following suggestions:

1. Find positives in your experiences. It's okay, and even healthy, to feel sadness, disappointment, anger, frustration and other unpleasant emotions: in *Chapter M: Mindfulness* we even looked at how important it is to "be in your emotions." It's not okay, though, to let your distress control you; finding positives during difficulties is a key part of your happiness prescription.

To change your viewpoint, consider the following examples:

Negative view of shortcomings	More helpful view of shortcomings
I'm no good at tennis	I'm just learning how to play the sport
I've got no patience	I'm working on being more patient, but I also appreciate my passion
I'm stuck in my job	I'm happy to have a job and to have the freedom to explore other options while I'm still employed

No one is perfect, and we all make mistakes. The key to optimism is maximizing your successes and learning from your failures. Everything that happens has both positive and negative aspects even in the toughest of times. The more you look for the positives, the easier it'll get to find them in the future and the happier you'll end up being.

2. Take a step back. For some people, negative thoughts come easily - especially if left unchecked. Occasionally, take a step back and pay attention to the messages your brain is sending. Are they helpful or damaging? How could you translate some of the more negative messages into something more optimistic, encouraging and motivating? As Dr. Seuss said, "Don't cry because it's over. Smile because it happened."

3. Be around positive people. Being with negative people can make *you* feel down, but spending time with optimistic people can cause some of their happiness to rub off. In fact, you don't even need to be with these people in person: just learning about others and keeping their optimistic endeavors in mind can enhance your happiness.

Consider Beverly Bronson. In 1999, this London native left the comforts of her New York City apartment to volunteer for an agency in Nepal helping children in the town of Kathmandu.

The day she planned to return home, she saw two boys aged two and five sitting outside their tin hut — disheveled and neglected. Heartbroken, she did the only thing she could: put them on her list to receive sponsorship from the agency she was working for.

Two months later, Beverly found herself back in Nepal. She saw the young boys again, but this time they looked even worse: they were visibly starving and only half dressed - the younger was wearing nothing but a filthy t-shirt. No sponsorship money had arrived.

After finding out from a local man that their mother had abandoned them, Beverly was terrified that they'd be abducted by child traffickers. "*I scooped them up and took them with me. I didn't know what was going to happen, but I know you can always find a solution.*"

With this optimism, she did eventually find an answer. Within two years of her first visit to Kathmandu, she founded Ghar Sita Mutu – House with a Heart, *a home for abandoned children, a training program for destitute women and an outreach program for needy families in Kathmandu, it provides shelter, food, clothing and education - among other resources.* "*Helping out these families makes me feel fantastic,*" *she says.*

What challenges has Beverly overcome? Many. Beverly is a woman of little means who strives to make ends meet in her own life. She lives in New York and owns a small antique store, so just getting to Nepal isn't easy. She has no prior experience of starting or running a nonprofit organization, and is not a huge fan of fundraising – something she has to do as she receives no governmental assistance. There's a huge communication barrier, too, because at the onset, Beverly spoke almost no Nepalese.

Despite these obstacles, her optimism, passion and determination have prevailed and drastically improved both her own life and that of many others.[14]

Beverly's story teaches us that, with a positive outlook, challenges are never too big to overcome. When we maintain realistic levels of optimism, our happiness increases even in the face of overwhelming odds.

---

14   Want to help Beverly with her mission? Visit www.gharsitamutu.com.

Name

Address   Date

℞ BE REALISTICALLY OPTIMISTIC

✓ Find positives in your experiences

✓ Take a step back to evaluate your passing thoughts and try to modify any negative thinking

✓ Surround yourself with positive people

Signature

P: PROBLEM SOLVING

ADDRESS PROBLEMS HEAD-ON

> Problems are like leaks: the longer you avoid
> them, the bigger the mess they become.

Living a happy life doesn't mean living one without problems
– these only exist in fairy tales. Happy people are just good at
coping with their problems.

Each day we face a wide array of problems: from smaller
difficulties such as, "None of my clothes are clean," or "There's
a long line at Starbucks and I'm already late for my meeting," to
larger problems like, "I can't pay my mortgage," or "My spouse
is having an affair."

Despite how often problems come up, not many of us
know how to effectively deal with them. Imagine a world where
everyone could successfully address issues with themselves, their
families, their organizations, their countries and even the entire
planet: sounds like a prescription for happiness to me!

My mentors, Drs. Arthur and Christine Nezu, have been
instrumental in teaching effective problem solving techniques
to individuals and groups around the globe. Th ey and their
colleagues have demonstrated the benefits of effectively coping
with difficulties, including:

- ✓ Less depression and anxiety
- ✓ Reduced stress
- ✓ Improved quality of life
- ✓ More self-confidence
- ✓ Better physical health
- ✓ Improved mood

The Diagnosis: Avoiding the issues

> *No problem can withstand the assault*
> *of sustained thinking.*
>
> **-Voltaire,**
> **French Philosopher**

Most of the difficulties that stem from life's challenges have little to do with the availability of solutions. Instead, our challenges turn into problems because we don't address what's at their hearts.

How do you tend to cope with problems? Are you more likely to:

- ✓ Avoid problems, hoping they'll disappear?
- ✓ Try impulsively to solve them as quickly as possible to get them eliminated?

If you're using either one of these approaches, you're not solving your problems as effectively as you could be.

Your Prescription: Tackle the issues

All the world is full of suffering;
It is also full of overcoming it.

-Helen Keller,
Author and Political Activist

Depending on the situation you face, solving a problem effectively can be challenging. Drs. Nezu and their colleagues have developed a five-step system to best deal with what life throws at you:

1. Develop a healthy mindset
2. Define your problem
3. Come up with lots of potential solutions
4. Chose the best solution
5. Follow through with your chosen solution and make sure it works

1. Develop a healthy mindset. The first step to solving a problem effectively is believing that you *can* overcome it with the proper amounts of time and effort. If you're committed to bettering your situation and have confidence in your ability to do so, you're combining realistic optimism with self-efficacy, resilience and hardiness. This greatly improves your chances of success.

When Sylvia first came to see me, she was extremely negative about her ability to make things better in her life. As an executive who had lost her job when her company downsized, she was so overwhelmed about her unemployment that she couldn't even think about looking for a new job - much less get her resume together and start the search.

Her stress level was so extreme that she couldn't sleep, was eating pounds of "comfort food" (leading to excessive pounds on her body), and was frequently arguing with her husband and children. "No one's going to hire me," she told me. "There's nothing I can do!"

In fact, there was a lot she could do, but first we needed her to believe in herself and adopt a more positive outlook. Before long, using some of the techniques found in Chapters B: Belief, O: Optimism and U: Understanding, *she was able to see that although the economy wasn't overly favorable for hiring, there were many things she could do to better her situation.*

2. Define your problem. In order to address a problem as best we can, we need to know what the problem is. Sometimes, what we first think is the issue is just a smaller part of the overall difficulty.

For Sylvia, she saw her unemployment as her "only" trouble. While this was definitely an important problem, there was also more going on - most notably her reaction to having lost a job: insomnia, irritability, overeating and paralysis from the overwhelming stress.

As we worked through this problem-solving step, Sylvia decided that the first problem to address was her high level of stress. This would be the key to making further improvements.

3. Come up with lots of potential solutions. Brainstorm to come up with as many potential solutions to your problems as possible. At this stage, it's best to just grab a pen and a blank piece of paper and start "free" writing without pausing to analyze what you wrote. The more ideas you get, the better. Don't worry about how good they are at this stage: just come up with as many as you can.

4. Choose the best solution. Once you've generated a variety of solutions, it's time to choose the most effective one. Assess the following criteria for each option:

✓ Will this actually solve the problem?
✓ Can I implement this solution (with help if needed)?

✓ What are the short-term consequences?
✓ What are the long-term consequences?
✓ What are the personal consequences?
✓ What are the social consequences to others (family, friends, society etc.)?

Now that you've evaluated your options, which one looks best? Is there a way to make it even better? For example, can you combine two pretty good ideas to make a great solution?

After completing Steps Three and Four, Sylvia decided to: (1) Address her stress by practicing daily relaxation exercises and changing her negative thinking, and (2) Speak with some recruiters who might be able to help her find a new job.

5. Follow through with the solution and make sure it works.
Implement the most effective solution (or solutions) you identify, and then verify that what you did was helpful.

Sometimes people come up with a great way to handle a problem but avoid following through with it, or decide to try an approach but never assess how helpful it really was. Performing and evaluating the chosen solution are vital components to effectively coping with problems.

Sylvia was able to reduce her stress using the techniques she implemented, and by doing so became better able to apply the advice she received from recruiters. Although she still didn't have a job, she knew that there were possibilities out there. She soon came to appreciate that, had she not gone though the problem solving steps, she would probably have been too overwhelmed to really focus on this next stage of her life.

In addition to making progress toward gaining employment, other aspects of her life were also improving: there were fewer arguments with her family, she was better able to sleep and she gave up her attempts at "food therapy."

As we see with Sylvia, effective problem solving can drastically decrease your stress levels - regardless of what's happening in your life. As it's sometimes said, "A bend in the road isn't the end of the road . . . unless you fail to make the turn." Use effective problem solving to make the most out of that turn.

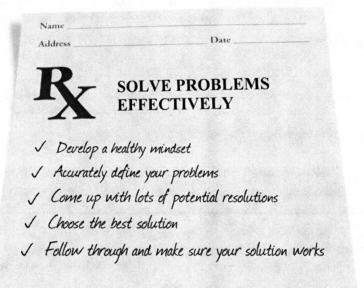

Name _____

Address _____ Date _____

R̶X SOLVE PROBLEMS EFFECTIVELY

✓ Develop a healthy mindset

✓ Accurately define your problems

✓ Come up with lots of potential resolutions

✓ Choose the best solution

✓ Follow through and make sure your solution works

Signature _____

Q: QUESTIONS

SPEND TIME QUESTIONING YOUR THOUGHTS

> Your thoughts are the most powerful predictors of your happiness and health.

How we think has a huge impact on how we feel and what we do as a result. This concept is well demonstrated by public speaking.

Known as "the number one fear" (even ahead of the fear of dying), stress associated with speaking in front of a crowd is extremely common. In my private practice, I've worked with many people, including CEOs, whose public speaking anxieties are severely hindering their business and personal lives. They've joined the likes of Madonna, Barbara Streisand, and Frank Sinatra (all frequent performers) who admitted to feeling anxious about getting on stage.

What causes this almost-universal fear? It's not usually the actual act of standing up before a group of people and speaking so much as it's about our expectations: our beliefs and perceptions of what the event will be like. In short, it's our thoughts that cause the fear.

Thoughts are explanations we provide ourselves for situations. During the course of the day, these messages unconsciously form our interpretations of events past, present and future. It's for this reason that they're called **automatic thoughts**.

Although we're not always aware of them, these can be extremely powerful. Consider, for example, how you might react if you were unexpectedly asked to give a presentation in front of two-hundred-and-fifty people tomorrow morning.

The first thing many people might notice would be a *physiological reaction*: increased heart rate, tight muscles, nausea or sweating. Common *emotions* include fear, anxiety, worry or even anger. *Behaviorally* you might decline the request, or agree to it but then stay up all night because you were too nervous to sleep.

What causes these intense physical, emotional and behavioral reactions are our automatic thoughts. Examples of these might include:

- ✓ I won't know what to say
- ✓ I'll look like a fool
- ✓ People will think I'm a complete idiot
- ✓ I'm going to mess up

Sometimes we're aware of such thoughts, but sometimes we're not.

When Maryann came to see me, she was so nervous about speaking in front of groups that she was having trouble sleeping weeks before a presentation. She was particularly afraid of messing up with her words at some point during the speech, but there was a bigger fear which eventually came out, that, "If I don't do this perfectly, I'll get fired."

The primary breadwinner in the household, losing her job would put a huge strain on her family. Before every speech (and her job required her to give quite a few), her automatic thoughts told her that failure was imminent. Like most of us in this situation, she didn't stop to question these thoughts - her brain just accepted them as truths. No wonder she was so stressed out!

Where do automatic thoughts come from? Th ey're a culmination of many different factors, including:

- ✓ **Past experiences** - from as long ago as childhood to as recently ago as one second
- ✓ **The environment** - what's happening around us and influencing our senses
- ✓ **Emotions** - how we feel emotionally
- ✓ **Physical sensations** - how we feel physically
- ✓ **The desire to make sense out of life** - making unconscious assumptions about why things happen

The Diagnosis: Unhelpful automatic thoughts

If you don't like something, change it. If you can't change it, change your attitude.

- Maya Angelou,
Poet, Activist, Actress and Speaker

Our brains serve up automatic thoughts with little consideration for their accuracy or usefulness. These assumptions can be divided into different categories, which are collectively known as **cognitive distortions.**

These refer to inaccurate and unhelpful thinking patterns that can lead to a host of unwanted emotions, physical discomforts and unhealthy behaviors.

The following table contains a list of five commonly used distortions. Do any of them sound familiar to you?

Distortion	What is it?	Example
All-or-nothing thinking	Thinking in absolute terms, often using *all, none, always, never, everyone, no one*	"No one understands me." "I'll never reach my goal."
Mindreading	Assuming you know what others are thinking without having adequate evidence of their thoughts	"He thinks I'm such a loser." "She doesn't think I can do this."
Fortune-telling	Predicting the future negatively: expecting bad things to happen	"Things are just going to get worse." "He's not going to call me."
"Should" thinking	Passing judgment by using the term "should" rather than simply stating objective facts	"I should be better at this." "He should text me if he really cares."
Blaming / personalizing	Placing all responsibility on others (blaming) or yourself (personalizing) while failing to acknowledge any role you or someone else may have had	Blaming: "It's all his fault we got divorced." Personalizing: "It's all my fault the project failed."

Your Prescription: Learn to question your thoughts

No man is happy who does not think himself so.

- Publilius Syrus,
Latin Writer during 1ˢᵗ Century BC

How we think affects how we feel and what we do. By questioning unhelpful thoughts, we can dramatically improve our lives as well as the lives of those around us.

Nobody drives this home better than Susan Davis. Starting off her career teaching special education, Susan worked with children with disabilities. During her time teaching, she learned to go against many traditional assumptions, including:

✓ *Parents with complex issues (such as medical or psychiatric illnesses) can't be good parents*
✓ *Teens make bad parents and should relinquish their babies*
✓ *An agency can only help a certain group of people (children OR parents, etc.) do a specific task (adoption, mental health OR assistance for moms before birth, etc.)*

In 1997, she founded Every Child, Inc. *out of her kitchen with the help of a few colleagues.[15] The organization now staffs over seventy-five people who, with an annual budget of approximately $4 million, try to address the specific needs of each child and family they work with. By refusing to accept what others took as facts, Susan and her team have succeed in helping over three-thousand children achieve a loving, lasting family relationship.*

As an example, let me tell you about Amy. In her twenties, Amy became pregnant. The pregnancy was complicated by a variety of factors – including her history of drug addiction, her depression and the baby's absent father.

Every Child Inc. *was first contacted by Amy's doctor before she was due when it became obvious that her baby was going to have serious health issues. They assigned someone to help support her before, during and after labor, and also helped address her other needs: helping her remain sober, getting her help for her depression, and offering emotional encouragement.*

Sadly, the baby died after three weeks. The agency supported Amy through this difficult time and continued to work with her after it, as well.

---

15   For more information on Every Child Inc., visit their website at www.everychildinc.org.

In fact, when Amy got pregnant again, she requested to work with the same person at Every Child Inc. *who had helped her before.*

Today, Amy is the mother of a healthy and beautiful boy. She remains sober and is also no longer depressed. Gainfully employed, she has started schooling to get a degree in nursing and says she wants to help people get though difficult times, just as Every Child Inc. *was there for her.*

The agency, which helps hundreds of people like Amy every year, exists because Susan Davis dared to question the assumptions which so many others so easily make.

Questioning ourselves and getting to the heart of our automatic thoughts can often be difficult. Some people recommend that we ignore negative thinking in order to have more joy. "If you want to be happy," they say, "just have happy thoughts." This approach doesn't work well, however, and can serve only as band-aid over a huge wound.

To enhance your happiness levels effectively, it's vital to address your thinking. Here are three steps to question your thoughts and bring more joy into your life as a result:

1. Learn your ABCs. Whenever you experience unwanted emotions, physical sensations or behaviors, stop and ask yourself, "What am I saying to myself that's causing this reaction?" That is, identify your ABCs:

A =	Activator (what happens prior to your reaction – the event itself)
B =	Belief (automatic thoughts about the event)
C =	Consequences (emotional, physical and behavioral reactions to the event)

While some people think it's the activator that determines their reaction (e.g., *"I yelled because he said that"*), it's really the *belief* that's the pivotal point.

Remember Roger who we met in the introduction - the man who lost both of his arms in an electrical accident? How might you react if you were faced with a similar situation? Let's look at the ABCs:

	Activator	Belief	Consequences
Roger's reaction	Both arms amputated	*"Despite the challenges, I know there's a positive reason for this accident."*	Feelings of hope and motivation; active participation in physical rehabilitation
How others might have reacted		*"My life's over. I can't do anything without my arms."*	Feelings of despair; staying in bed and refusing to do physical therapy

Depending on our automatic thoughts, we can have drastically different reactions to the same events. It's important to identify your beliefs because *they're* the things which trigger your responses – not the events themselves.

2. Identify your distortions. Assess the accuracy and helpfulness of your automatic thoughts. Go through the list of distortions presented earlier in the chapter to determine which ones you might be using.

3. Get some new thoughts. Once you've identified your thoughts and distortions, it's time to change inaccurate and unhelpful thinking. Develop a list of counter-thoughts that are helpful and truthful: beliefs you want to believe - even if you don't believe them yet.

To illustrate these last two steps, let's return to the example from the beginning of the chapter regarding speaking in front of two-hundred-and-fifty people:

Automatic thought	Cognitive distortion	New, more helpful thought
I'll look like a fool	Fortune-telling	I'll practice and do my best
People will think I'm a complete idiot if I mess up	Mindreading	If I do mess up, people will likely empathize with me more than think negatively of me
I always forget everything I'm supposed to say	All-or-nothing thinking	Even if I forget exactly what I want to say, I know the concepts well enough to move on

Consider how you'd feel if you believed the more accurate and helpful thoughts in the third column. Probably a lot happier, right? Practice questioning your thoughts on a daily basis.

This is such a crucial step to enhancing your happiness that I've developed some forms to help you really focus on it. You can download them for free at www.ahappyyou.com.

Name _____

Address _____ Date _____

R℞ QUESTION YOUR THOUGHTS

✓ Question the accuracy of your thoughts

✓ Learn your ABCs: Activators, Beliefs and Consequences

✓ Identify and eliminate distortions

✓ Replace counter productive thoughts with new, more empowering ones

Signature _____

R: RELAXATION

RELAX YOUR WAY TO HAPPINESS

> Relaxation is a powerful but underused tool that can counteract stress and its unwanted consequences (overeating, procrastination, insomnia, discontent etc.).

The word **relaxation** conjures up different images for different people: some might visualize sitting on the beach with a cool drink and good book, and others might imagine going for a jog. Regardless of your definition, relaxation can have amazing benefits on your level of happiness.

Relaxing doesn't require you to sit in an uncomfortable, cross-legged position and repeatedly hum "om," either. True relaxation, in which you flush the stress out of your body and mind, is just a simple way of being happier.

Despite its powerful nature, relaxation is often not part of our everyday lives. Instead, its nemesis, stress, is much more common. Stress can adversely affect our bodies, feelings and behaviors. Here are some examples:

Physical effects of stress:

- ✓ Digestive problems
- ✓ Tight muscles
- ✓ Low/no energy
- ✓ Nervous/fidgety behavior
- ✓ Cardiac problems
- ✓ Headaches
- ✓ Frequent colds
- ✓ High blood pressure
- ✓ Rapid/shallow breathing
- ✓ Perspiration
- ✓ Dizziness

Emotional effects of stress:

- ✓ Sadness
- ✓ Anger
- ✓ Helplessness
- ✓ Hopelessness
- ✓ Frustration
- ✓ Worry
- ✓ Fear
- ✓ Worthlessness
- ✓ Anxiety
- ✓ Guilt
- ✓ Resentment
- ✓ Shame
- ✓ Embarrassment

Cognitive effects of stress:

- ✓ Increased use of distorted/ inaccurate thinking
- ✓ Memory problems[16]
- ✓ Difficulty concentrating
- ✓ Stifled creativity

Behavioral effects of stress:

- ✓ Insomnia/too much sleep
- ✓ Overeating/ neglecting to eat
- ✓ Short temper
- ✓ Social withdrawal
- ✓ Smoking
- ✓ Drinking
- ✓ Illicit drug use
- ✓ Abuse of prescription drugs
- ✓ Procrastination
- ✓ Excessive crying

---

16   Interestingly, the hippocampus, responsible for certain memories, actually shrinks in size when you experience enduring stress.

Do any of these sound familiar? If so, stress could be at the heart of many of your problems. Not only are these results of stress, but they can also cause more tension, too. Each symptom adds more stress to your life and can have a serious effect on your levels of happiness.

The Diagnosis: Being stressed out

For fast-acting relief, try slowing down.

**-Lily Tomlin,
Actress and Comedian**

Stress is sometimes called "the silent killer," because low levels of it can go virtually unnoticed before manifesting into serious health conditions or behavioral problems like the ones listed above.

So, how stressed out are you? On a scale from 0-10, with 0 being "no stress" and 10 being "the most stressed out you've ever been," how stressed out are you right now?

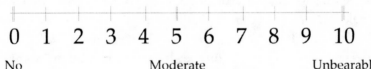

| 0 | 1 | 2 | 3 | 4 | 5 | 6 | 7 | 8 | 9 | 10 |

No
Stress

Moderate
Stress

Unbearable
Stress

What increases that number? What decreases it?

There are many quick remedies available to significantly reduce your stress levels and increase happiness, but in this chapter, we'll focus on relaxation exercises.

Your Prescription: Prioritize daily relaxation

There must be quite a few things that a hot bath won't cure,
but I don't know many of them.

-Sylvia Plath,
Poet and Novelist

Whether you have three minutes or three hours, there are many ways you can incorporate relaxation into your day. The "best" relaxation depends on the individual and varies from person to person. Below is a selection of ways to promote deep relaxation of the mind and body. Choose the method(s) that best fit your lifestyle, personality and time constraints:

1. Deep breathing. When asked what THE one step people could take to enhance their overall wellness is, mind-body guru Dr. Andrew Weil emphatically responds: proper breathing.

How do you do it? Place a hand over your diaphragm, which is situated above your bellybutton. Each time you inhale (bring air in), you want the diaphragm to expand. You'll know this is happening when your hand rises with your breath. When you exhale (let air out), your hand will sink.

You can do this at any time: when you're in traffic, at a meeting or getting ready for bed. It may seem a bit awkward at first, but the more you practice it, the easier it will get and the more relaxing it will become.

2. Progressive muscle relaxation. Progressive muscle relaxation involves systematically relaxing specific areas of the body. You might start with your toes and move up your body, or start at the top of your head and progress downward - releasing muscle tension in each area.[17]

---

17   Visit www.ahappyyou.com for more information about this and other relaxation practices.

3. **Meditation**. Meditation is about focusing on a particular vision, sound, word, movement or object while ignoring other stimuli. Doing this for even five minutes a day can greatly reduce your stress levels. If your mind wanders off to something negative, simply redirect your attention back to your meditative activity.

4. **Visualization.** Is your brain spinning too much to focus on meditation? Visualization is another great way to refocus negative energy and channel peaceful thoughts. Visualize a relaxing, joyful scenario in your mind to distract yourself from your life's tensions. This could be a favorite vacation spot, a happy memory or a picture of yourself achieving your biggest goal: no matter what you choose to visualize, focus on something positive and happy. Use all of your senses - sight, sound, smell, taste and touch - to bring the picture to life and to escape from stress.

5. **Massage.** There are various types of massage, from therapeutic to deep tissue. By working out muscular tension, you can relax both your mind and body. Massage is a great relaxation aid for increasing your happiness.

6. **Yoga**. Yoga was originally developed by Hindu priests as a course of physical and mental exercises for liberating yourself from the material world. It involves a series of postures and breathing exercises used to achieve a natural union of mind, body and spirit.

All of these relaxation methods can help your mind and body take a short break from the stresses in your life. Consider the following examples:

✓ *With a self-described "Type A" personality, Sue Oliver was dealing with a lot: her father's terminal cancer, her own divorce and a high-pressure job in corporate America. Her heightened stress resulted in little sleep, poor eating habits and isolation from her friends. After incorporating meditation into her daily routine, however, she explains, "I realized that I don't have to be carried away by any stress, and my life's never been the same."*

✓ *Barbara Zamost was an avid runner for almost thirty years when she developed what she describes as, "full-blown asthma. I couldn't run more than a few yards without gasping for air and feeling my heart race with panic." She took medication, but then started practicing diaphragmatic breathing and yoga. Since applying these relaxation practices, she's off the asthma medication, is breathing freely and is again exercising without problems.*

✓ *After getting into a car accident and suffering horrible pain, Anita Lopez turned to yoga. This is how she described her experience: "The relaxing effects it's had on my body, my mind and my spirit have been amazing. I am truly giddy - happy all the time because I'm cool, calm and collected . . . and it's no joke. People think I'm 'seriously not that happy', but I am!" In fact, this former television anchor loved it so much that she started teaching yoga to others with her own program - AnitaYoga.[18]*

✓ *In addition to the stress of planning a wedding, Natasha Sunshine-Antonioni and her fiancé were renovating their future home. Each had their own (passionate) opinions about how it should look, and this led to a fair amount of tension between them: "I would be in the kitchen steaming about how I wasn't sure if I could spend my life with a man like this," Natasha recalls. Then she started gratitude meditation where she focused on her fiancé's many positive aspects. Not only did it help her and her partner get through some challenging times, but it continues to be beneficial to their relationship today: "Six years later, I can say this is a key practice I have carried through my marriage."*

---

18   For more information on Anita Lopez, visit her website at www.anitayoga.net.

Think of relaxation as pushing a "reset" button in your psyche so stress doesn't build up. Practicing any of these activities will make a noticeable difference in your mood, your ability to handle life and your overall satisfaction. You'll be able to face new challenges head-on without feeling overwhelmed by stress.

Name _____

Address _____ Date _____

Rx MAKE RELAXATION A PRIORITY

✓ Incorporate relaxation methods into your daily life

✓ Do deep breathing

✓ Perform progressive muscle relaxation exercises

✓ Meditate

✓ Visualize your way to relaxation

✓ Get a massage

✓ Practice yoga

Signature _____

S: SONGS

USE MUSIC TO MAKE YOURSELF HAPPY

> Music can motivate and relax: it can give you
> a break from the challenges of life as well as
> enhance already enjoyable experiences.

Songs, and music in general, can have a profound impact on our moods. Moviemakers capitalize on this; when I was younger, the only way I could watch *Jaws* or *Halloween* was by plugging my ears because the music was what was most scary for me (now I simply can't watch horror films at all!). Also consider the energy you experience when you hear the theme song from *Rocky*.

Another emotion music can bring about is happiness – and that's what this chapter is all about.

The Diagnosis: No rhythm

Music was my refuge. I could crawl into the space between the notes and curl my back to loneliness.

- Maya Angelou,
Poet , Activist, Actress and Speaker

If you've got a headache, what do you do? Many people reach for an aspirin or another over-the-counter medication. Using this logic, does a *lack* of aspirin cause a headache? Of course not - but it can help make a headache better. Similarly, a lack of music in your life may not cause unhappiness, but incorporating melody into your day can inspire joy.

Incorporating music into your life can:

Enhance	Lessen
✓ Relaxation	✓ Stress
✓ Creative thinking	✓ Pain
✓ Communication	✓ Depression
✓ Mind and body wellness	✓ Anxiety
✓ Motivation and energy	✓ Insomnia

There are other benefits to music, too: ever wish you could get the "runner's high" without breaking a sweat? Apparently, you can. One study found that music offered similar psychological effects to exercising. Unfortunately, the *physical* benefits of listening to music aren't the same as they are for working out!

Cynde Huebner is an excellent example of how music can bring greater happiness. As a child, Cynde and her family moved every year for her father's job. Due to this, and the fact that she was painfully shy, she describes her childhood as one with, "no friends. I felt like a worm that shouldn't have been born." Wow.

She vividly remembers an incident in the second grade that scarred her for life. Her town was hosting a concert where all the students from the ten area grade schools would perform. For some reason, however, Cynde was cut from the performance.

"I was devastated," she explains, "and I bore this shame all by myself, quietly, for decades." To her, being told she wasn't good enough to sing at the concert equated to being told she wasn't good enough, period. Her self-confidence, already low, plummeted.

Over the years, she felt a strong desire to play the piano, but the experience from her past kept her from trying. That all changed, though, one day in the summer of 2008 when she learned about a program called Simply Music. *Developed by musician Neil Moore,* Simply Music *is a revolutionary approach to teaching music that pledges: "Students from all ages are playing great-sounding pieces immediately from their first lessons." As she describes, "I thought it sounded kind of hokey, but I decided to give it a try."*

The results of this program have been remarkable. Not only has Cynde learned to play the piano, but she has reaped a host of other benefits, too. Her self-confidence increased so much, for example, that she was soon able to give piano recitals in front of family and friends – playing classics, a song she had written herself, and even singing Amazing Grace!

She describes this musical outlet as having drastically changed her life for the better. In addition to the self-confidence she's gained, music helps her be more creative, relieve stress, express herself and experience hope. For Cynde, incorporating music into her life has brought delight and joy she never thought possible.

Your Prescription: Rejoice in music

I think I should have no other mortal wants if I could always have plenty of music. It seems to infuse strength into my limbs and ideas into my brain. Life seems to go on without effort when I am filled with music.

- George Eliot,
Pen Name of Mary Ann Evans, Novelist

So, how can you follow Cynde's example and enhance your happiness with music? Try the following suggestions:

1. Try different music media. Both listening to and creating music can enhance your joy, so why not try both? We'll focus on *listening* to music below, so let's look at *making* music here.

Creating music may mean singing a tune, writing a song or playing a melody. Don't think you're good enough to do this? That's the beauty: it doesn't matter. Unless you'll be performing on stage at the Kennedy Center (or somewhere similar), your actual abilities aren't an issue. All that's important is giving yourself the opportunity to create music without judging or being critical of what you produce. Enjoy the musical journey.

2. Listen to what you like. Think you have to listen to classical music to relax? Th ink again. A study entitled *Perceived and physiological indicators of relaxation: As different as Mozart and Alice in Chains* demonstrates that self-selected music has greater benefits than listening to conventional "relaxation" music. So long as you enjoy it, listen to what you want!

3. Use the music you need at that time. Different music can help us in different ways. Listen to music that will get you into the state you desire - whether it be to relax, to become more energetic, to get motivated, to be creative, to lessen your distress or to just find more joy.

Ever experience road rage? One study found that listening to your favorite music can even help reduce the stress caused by traffic.

4. Listen to positive songs. When looking at music to choose, consider different aspects about the tune: the beat, volume and lyrics. While many songs have may have a great beat, some of their lyrics are less than positive - and sometimes even degrading. Listen to music that empowers you with positive messages. Classic examples include:

- ✓ *Walking on Sunshine* by Katrina & The Waves
- ✓ *Beautiful* by Christina Aguilera
- ✓ *Survivor* by Beyoncé Knowles
- ✓ *Unwritten* by Natasha Bedingfield

Name _____

Address _____ Date _____

℞ USE MUSIC TO BOOST YOUR HAPPINESS

✓ Incorporate music into your life

✓ Create some music yourself

✓ Listen to the music you like _ not the music you think you "should" like

✓ Use the music you need at the time

✓ Listen to positive songs

Signature _____

T: TALKING

TALK YOUR WAY TO SATISFACTION

> Effective communication is an under-practiced dance that can propel your happiness to levels you might have never thought possible.

Remember the game "telephone" where one person whispers a message into another's ear, who then whispers the message to the next person? This ensemble continues until the last person recites what they heard out loud. The final message usually comes out something like "My shoe's in ink for my love" or some other nonsensical sentence that isn't even close to the original statement.

This game is a classic example of muddled communication. Despite what we say, people often hear something very different.

In the game of "telephone," the results of faulty informational transmission are humorous. In real life, however, poor communication can mean stress, strained relationships, missed opportunities, wasted efforts and general unhappiness.

On the other hand, effective communication can decrease stress, improve relationships, help you capitalize on opportunities, save time and energy and propel your happiness. As we'll see later, it might even save your life!

The Diagnosis: Being passive or aggressive

Two monologues do not make a dialogue.

-Jeff Daly,
Chief Designer of the
Metropolitan Museum of Art

How effective is your communication style? Which approach best describes your interactions when things aren't going as you'd like?

A. You don't speak up for yourself because you don't want to hurt other people's feelings or are afraid of their reactions. As a result, you keep your thoughts and feelings inside.
B. You stick up for your rights at all costs - even if that means interrupting others or raising your voice.
C. You don't outwardly communicate your concerns, but your irritation comes out passively through your behavior.
D. You confidently and respectfully bring up issues and try to resolve them peacefully with others.

Passive (A), **aggressive** (B) and **passive-aggressive** (C) interactions tend not to be effective means of communication, but being **assertive** (D) can enhance happiness. These communication styles are outlined in the following table:

	Individual doesn't respect others	Individual respects others
Individual doesn't clearly stand up for own rights	Passive-aggressive (C)	Passive (A)
Individual clearly stands up for own rights	Aggressive (B)	Assertive (D)

Assertiveness refers to effective communication that permits you to express your beliefs clearly while still respecting others. When you're assertive, there's a greater likelihood of happiness for both sides of the communication.

Your Prescription: Be assertive

> *The problem with communication . . . is the illusion that it has been accomplished.*
>
> **-George Bernard Shaw, Nobel Prize-Winning Author and Playwright**

Regardless of where you are now, you can learn to be a more effective communicator. Use the following five steps to enhance your interactions as well as your happiness:

1. Be assertive. Speak up for yourself while being respectful toward others:

Want a pay raise?
Confidently explain to your boss why you think you deserve one.

Not crazy about your new haircut?
Tell your hairdresser and see what can be done.

Upset that your friend incessantly complains about her
husband when you wish you had one to grumble about?
Let her know.

Give yourself permission to value yourself as well as others.
Despite assumptions (e.g. "she should know that upsets me"), no
one can read your mind. Express yourself while listening to and
respecting others.

2. Identify and share your feelings. Keeping your feelings
bottled up from those who are closest to you is a major obstacle
to health and happiness.

In fact, suppressing your emotions is a predictor of a shorter
life span; a study following almost four-thousand people for a
decade found that women who "self-silenced" during conflict
with their spouse were four times more likely to die then women
who openly communicated their thoughts and feelings. These
results were independent of a variety of factors that might
influence death - including chronic medical illness, obesity and
smoking.

Additional benefits of sharing your feelings with others can
include closer relationships, decreased stress and enhanced self-
esteem. While I'm not suggesting you go overboard by telling
your significant other, boss, friend or children *everything* that's
on your mind, open communication is vital to good health and
happiness.

3. Examine your thoughts. If you could stick a microphone in
your brain, what would you hear yourself thinking? Consider
your thoughts *before* you speak to avoid making a statement that
you'll regret later. If you need help with this, refer to *Chapter Q:
Questions.*

As an example, watch out for automatic thoughts such as "I have to be right" or "I have to win this argument." While we may not realize it, these types of beliefs are not usually helpful: they cause us to keep pushing the other party while tuning out what they're saying. If you're correct, accept it and move on without needing to have others acknowledge it.

In general, remember that different opinions do not mean that one is right and the other is wrong: both points are likely to have some merit.

4. Ask questions and listen. The art of communicating effectively involves listening as well as speaking up. Just improving your listening skills will make you a better communicator - both in your work and your personal life.

Try having a conversation with someone where most of your comments are questions or reflective listening (e.g. "sounds like you had a rough day"). You might be surprised at the wealth of information you learn, and the person you're communicating with is also likely to appreciate your devoted interest to what they're saying!

5. Express your appreciation. Often, our dialogues focus on conveying negative feedback (e.g. a "what's broken now?" mentality). Imagine how different you might feel if your conversation concentrated on positives. The following ideas are good ways to get started:

- ✓ Thank a loved one for their support
- ✓ Appreciate a co-worker for assisting you on a project
- ✓ Express gratitude to someone serving you (at a store, restaurant etc.)

You'll be amazed how far these simple acts of effective communication can go in enhancing your own happiness.

To illustrate the significance of communicating effectively, let's look at the life of David Novak. David is CEO of Yum! Brands *and author of* The Education of an Accidental CEO: Lessons Learned from the Trailer Park to the Corner Office. *Throughout his book and seminars, David emphasizes the importance of communication in both personal interactions and the business culture at large.*

David grew up poor and dislocated; he'd lived in thirty-two different trailer parks in twenty-three states by the time he was thirteen. Despite his poverty and lack of a formal business degree, however, he rose to become CEO of the largest restaurant company in the world - with an average compensation of $14 million a year.

How does he manage a company with over thirty-five-thousand locations and literally a million employees? Direct communication.

For example, each year the company runs a three-day training program for managers. David heads the program himself, and shares personal stories from his own experiences. "Doing so makes a big company seem small," he says. Each manager is also expected to know the aims, strategies and overall spirit of the company, and every supervisor is encouraged to recognize excellence in others.

Not only does David encourage his team to reinforce positive behaviors, but he also embraces the act of appreciation himself. In fact, he's developed his own award (a pair of smiling teeth) that he gives out to reward specific employees for their extraordinary work.

This seasoned CEO has learned from experience how to strike a balance that avoids aggression and passivity. Although his managers and friends describe him as "hyper-competitive" and "driven to win," his management style emphasizes effective interactions, teamwork, commitment and respect.

You can't help but notice the big smile on his own face, either: David's communication skills have not just made him successful — they've also made him happier.

Try new, effective approaches to communication and see where you get: I'm sure your happiness, as well as the contentment of those around you, will grow.

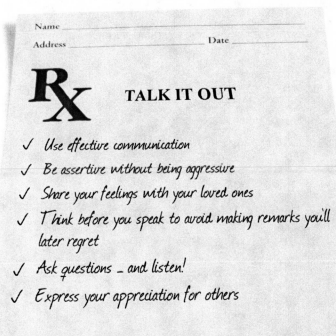

Name _____

Address _____ Date _____

R̞x̞   TALK IT OUT

✓ *Use effective communication*

✓ *Be assertive without being aggressive*

✓ *Share your feelings with your loved ones*

✓ *Think before you speak to avoid making remarks you'll later regret*

✓ *Ask questions – and listen!*

✓ *Express your appreciation for others*

Signature _____

U: UNDERSTANDING

UNDERSTAND, ACCEPT AND EMBRACE CHA

> Embrace, rather than fear, change.
> If you do, better days will follow.

Change is a constant in our lives. Sometin
sometimes it's difficult and painful, and still ot
something we really want and then feel bad for w
happen.

Despite its universal presence, however, it's rar
to deal with it effectively. Imagine a world where
able to embrace change: I'm sure happiness and a
would follow.

The Diagnosis: Resisting change

Change is hard because people overestimate the v
have—and underestimate the v
may gain (

— **James Belasco a**
In their book *Flig*

It's not always easy to cope with change. Most of us have experienced this difficulty with major life challenges - such as the following:

- ✓ Divorce
- ✓ Losing a loved one
- ✓ Illness
- ✓ Income change

- ✓ Becoming unemployed
- ✓ Losing a competition

Change can also be difficult to cope with when it's something you want - as with the following examples:

- ✓ Getting married
- ✓ Having a baby
- ✓ Starting a new job

- ✓ Getting a new roommate
- ✓ Moving to a new town

When we feel that we can't change a situation (either because we've got no control over it or because there are reasons why it's important for it to happen), we can feel powerless, hopeless and unsure as to how we should go forward.

These are normal feelings, however, so don't worry about them. Fortunately, your prescription for happiness includes how to understand and embrace change.

Your Prescription: Accept and embrace change

It is not necessary to change. Survival is not mandatory.

**-W. Edwards Deming,
Statistician and Innovator**

Change is one of life's inevitable occurrences, but there are many ways to handle it — collectively known as **resilience**. When

you are resilient, you learn to accept what's happening and to excel: it's a great way of boosting your happiness.

Dr. Julie Smith, CEO of LifePath, has developed a five-step process to help people become more change-resilient. Her book series, *When 'It' Happens!*, teaches people how to better cope with whatever life throws at them.

In the series, she refers to certain responses to change which she calls "locked." These responses prevent you from moving forward effectively. Conversely, what she calls "unlocked" responses help you to cope with change well and lead to more joy and contentment.

Here are Dr. Smith's five steps to best coping with change:

1. Overcome negative feelings that come with change
2. Reframe unproductive thoughts
3. Try new behaviors
4. Arrange encouraging consequences to keep yourself motivated
5. Discover the impact you have on others as you deal with change

Step 1: Overcome negative feelings that come with change

What's preventing effective coping with change?	*Locked feelings* - such as feeling hopeless, helpless, and being overwhelmed
What can help you better deal with the change?	*Unlocked feelings* - such as courage and empowerment
How can you unlock your feelings?	Overcome negative feelings by identifying them and getting them out in a healthy way
Example	*For over four years, Heather had been taking care of her mother who had Alzheimer's: an overwhelming task both physically and emotionally. Over time, she began to feel hopeless, depressed and angry with her situation – especially with her siblings. "They don't give me any help," she said.* *As we worked together, however, Heather was able to identify her locked feelings more quickly and change them into more constructive, unlocked emotions. She did this by focusing on having more motivating feelings: how empowered she felt by all the different choices she could make; how grateful she felt for this time with her mother; how peaceful she felt when she accepted her situation.* *This led her into feeling much less stress and much greater happiness - despite the continuing challenges of caring for an aging parent.*

Step 2: Reframe unproductive thoughts

What's preventing effective coping with change?	*Locked thoughts* - such as "There's nothing I can do" or "My life's doomed."
What can help you better deal with the change?	*Unlocked thoughts* - such as "Although I didn't ask for this, I do have control over my reaction to it"
How can you unlock your thinking?	Reframe unproductive thoughts by looking for positives in tough situations and being grateful for what you still have
Example	*While walking to see a movie with her daughter, Dr. Fern Kazlow (known as Dr. K) slipped and fell on a speed bump. This seemingly innocuous event changed her life.*
	The fall resulted in various fractures throughout her body - leaving her initially unable even to get out of bed. Her pain and disability didn't stop her, however; Dr. K's mindset got her through.
	"From the beginning I asked myself: 'How can I use this to grow me?' Whenever a situation is difficult, I find a way to learn – for myself and for others. I was determined not to define myself or be defined by my limitations. I accepted the reality of what had happened and the pain and constraints I was dealing with, but refused to get stuck on that story.
	"People identify themselves by their story - what they tell themselves about their life and their situation. I took this opportunity to look at what really mattered to me: my children and helping others in my work. I realized I could do a great deal right from my bed - including spending time with both of my children and consulting with clients by phone."
	Dr. K's unlocked thoughts helped, and continue to help, her to cope with her physical challenges.[19]

---

19   To learn more about Dr. K's "Shattering Financial Limitations™" visit http://www.drfernkazlow.com/

Step 3: Try new behaviors

What's preventing effective coping with change?	*Locked behaviors* - such as blaming others, arguing with others, resisting change through avoidance and sabotage
What can help you better deal with the change?	*Unlocked behaviors* - such as taking responsibility for dealing with your situation, asking for help or helping others
How can you unlock your behaviors?	Try new behaviors that help you move forward and adjust to the change
Example	*Montel Williams lives with multiple sclerosis and its resulting excruciating neuropathies: "It literally feels like you're taking a fork and stabbing me," he says.* *Rather than sit around sulking, however, Montel proactively does what he can to improve his life. He's now learned self-hypnosis, practices gratitude, exercises regularly and reaches out to help others - all of which help improve his pain and mood. He's a great role model for anyone facing significant challenges.*

Step 4: Arrange encouraging consequences to keep yourself motivated

What's preventing effective coping with change?	*Locked consequences* - such as getting pity from others
What can help you better deal with the change?	*Unlocked consequences* - such as patting yourself on the back for positive changes you make
How can you unlock positive consequences?	Find encouragement by surrounding yourself with a support group, by doing things that are rewarding or by encouraging yourself
Example	*After taking Apple computers from just an idea with a friend to a $2 billion company, Steve Jobs was fired from the job he loved. This was a devastating event that might have sent others into hiding, but not Steve.* *"I didn't see it then, but it turned out that getting fired from Apple was the best thing that could have ever happened to me," said Jobs, at age fifty. "It freed me up to enter one of the most creative periods in my life."* *Steve used this creativity to develop even more amazing projects, including Pixar (the first computer animated feature film company) and NeXT, which was later bought by Apple. He chose to engage in behaviors that resulted in positive consequences (using his creativity, doing what he loved). As a result, he and the people around him enjoyed significant happiness.*

Step 5: Discover the impact you have on others as you deal with change

What's preventing effective coping with change?	*Locked impact* on others by performing unhelpful behaviors that drive them away - such as being unfaithful
What can help you better deal with the change?	*Unlocking impact* on others by bringing loved ones closer - such as being honest
How can you unlock your impact on others?	Note your impact on others to learn why they might be attracted to you or want to avoid you
Example	*A previous client, Sara, came to see me while she was going through divorce proceedings with her husband of twelve years. She was feeling very lonely and scared.* *When asked about her social support, Sara emphatically responded that she couldn't count on anyone. She explained, "no one even calls to see how I'm doing."* *With further questioning, however, it appeared that the lack of support was more of an interpretation than a reality. When she really thought back, she could recount dozens of times when friends, family and co-workers had asked Sara to join them - out for a meal, over at their home or on a walk. Each time, she had declined.* *As a result of consistent "failures" to get her to come out, her social support had retreated - most likely trying to give her the space they thought she wanted.* *Sara decided to change her behavior that was having these negative effects on her loved ones: she started to call some friends and invite them out to dinner; she started to take a class with a co-worker; she accepted invitations to people's houses.* *Consequently, she experienced much less distress and loneliness. The social support she was now open to receiving helped her get through a difficult time - and even to find some joy.*

Dr. Smith's five steps show you how to be resilient in effectively dealing with change. Accepting and embracing change is a key to coping with the difficulties of an ever-changing existence. Master it and you'll handle your life's events better - and experience less stress and more happiness at the same time.

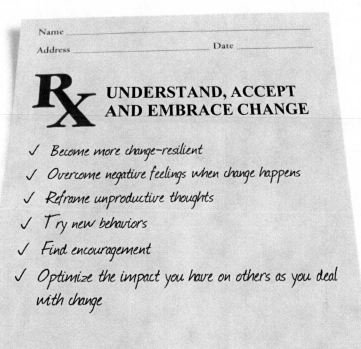

Name _____

Address _____ Date _____

R℞ UNDERSTAND, ACCEPT AND EMBRACE CHANGE

✓ Become more change-resilient

✓ Overcome negative feelings when change happens

✓ Reframe unproductive thoughts

✓ Try new behaviors

✓ Find encouragement

✓ Optimize the impact you have on others as you deal with change

Signature _____

V: VALUES

APPLY YOUR VALUES AND LEVERAGE YOUR STRENGTHS

> Show me a happy woman and I'll show you someone who uses her unique values and strengths in her life every day.

Values are characteristics we deem to be intrinsically positive - including virtues that we tend to label as "good." **Strengths** refer to qualities that make us unique. Your strengths include your values as well as your specific talents, knowledge and innate abilities. When our thoughts and behaviors coincide with our values and strengths, we're more likely to experience happiness.

Ever met someone who was happy in a career that you couldn't even imagine doing for ten minutes? That person was probably able to use her strengths (which are different from yours) in her work. Hopefully you're able to do so, too (or will be by the time you finish this chapter).

Identifying and applying strengths will enhance your happiness regardless of what's going on in your life. But how exactly can we do this?

In my practice, I often encourage my clients to start by completing a questionnaire called *Values-In-Action (VIA)* developed by Dr. Martin Seligman and Christopher Peterson. This inventory provides a comprehensive assessment of the virtues and strengths listed below:

Virtues	Strengths
Wisdom and Knowledge	Curiosity Love of learning Judgment Ingenuity Social intelligence Perspective
Courage	Bravery Perseverance Integrity and honesty
Humanity and Love	Kindness and generosity Loving and allowing yourself to be loved
Justice	Loyalty Fairness Leadership
Temperance	Self-control Prudence Humility
Transcendence	Appreciation of beauty and excellence Gratitude Hope Spirituality Forgiveness Playfulness and humor Passion and enthusiasm

The Diagnosis: Forgetting your values and not leveraging your strengths

Happiness is that state of consciousness which proceeds from the achievement of one's values.

**-Ayn Rand,
Author and Philosopher**

Much of the dissatisfaction, discontent and distress we experience in our lives doesn't come because we lack values or strengths, but because we don't apply them.

In addition to completing the VIA, you can also identify your specific values and strengths by answering the following questions:

- ✓ What do you enjoy doing, and what would you be doing more of if you had more free time?
- ✓ Are you frequently complimented for anything?
- ✓ Do you possess a skill that others lack?
- ✓ What makes you feel happiest and "in the zone"?
- ✓ What comes naturally to you?
- ✓ What makes you different from others?
- ✓ What are the five most important values to you?

Your Prescription: Use your gifts

Success is achieved by developing our strengths, not by eliminating our weaknesses.

**-Marilyn vos Savant,
"Ask Marilyn" Columnist**

Many successful people tend to capitalize on their strong points and minimize their weaknesses. The same goes for people who are happy; life becomes easier when you're "swimming with the current" (using your strengths) instead of constantly "swimming upstream" (not using them).

For a great example of someone who has capitalized on applying her values and strengths, we need look no further than daytime television:

Oprah Winfrey came from a challenging background: she was born into severe poverty and repeatedly abused as a child. Anyone else in her situation would probably have struggled just to survive in today's world, but Oprah has thrived to become one of the most successful icons in the world.

Although Oprah didn't even own a pair of shoes until she was six years old, she always had a gift for communicating with others. When she was only three years old, she could read - and later even wrote her kindergarten teacher a note explaining why she should be skipped to the first grade. This gift for speaking to others on both an informative and emotional level led her to become one of the youngest news anchors in the nation at the age of nineteen.

Capitalizing on her values and strengths, Oprah's life has been filled with much prosperity: her talk show is perhaps the most watched TV show in the world; she was the third woman to own her own production studio; she now has her own television network (OWN: The Oprah Winfrey Network).

In addition to an astronomical self-made net worth, her success is demonstrated by the millions of lives she's changed for the better via her charitable work, her media appearances and just by being herself. By applying her strengths, Oprah exudes joy and has brought immeasurable happiness all over the world.

Now ask yourself this: how can *you* maximally implement your values and core strengths in your daily life? Although there are major changes that can do this (switching jobs, for instance), there are also less radical modifications you can make, including:

1. Identify your top values and strengths. First, identify the core components of who you are:

✓ Try Seligman and Peterson's *Values-In-Action (VIA)*[20]
✓ Ask yourself the questions presented in the previous section
✓ Go to www.ahappyyou.com for a list of values and identify the five most important characteristics for you

2. Look for new ways to incorporate your values and strengths into your work and play. Once you know what your values and strengths are, use them in your everyday life: at home, at work, socially and during your "you" time. For example:

If this is one of your values or strengths . . .	. . . then try these:
Curiosity	Read something intriguing fifteen minutes before bed each night; take a class to learn something new
Empathy	Spend time with a friend or coworker who could use a caring ear; volunteer
Spirituality	Get up ten minutes early to read a spiritual book, pray or meditate
Humor	Sign up for a joke-of-the day email; schedule a lunch with a friend or coworker who makes you laugh
Family	Schedule a family breakfast before everyone's day starts; text each other during the day to see how everyone is doing

---

20   Find Seligman and Peterson's *Values-In-Action* at *www.authentichappiness. sas.upenn.edu*

Consider Millard Dean Fuller: a businessman, lawyer and self-made millionaire before he turned thirty. Despite his wealth, Millard was unhappy; he wasn't applying his core values. To combat this, he decided to change.

Millard and his wife gave up all of their wealth to focus on their values: family, empathy, spirituality, stewardship and kindness. They then started building houses for people who couldn't afford this part of the "American dream."

Over three-hundred-thousand houses later, Habitat for Humanity, *started by Millard and his family, is still going strong. As Millard once said, "It's not your blue blood, your pedigree or your college degree. It's what you do with your life that counts."*

3. Let go of activities that don't capitalize on your strengths. When possible, release any activity that you approach with a feeling of dread or procrastination. Why waste time on tasks that you don't really enjoy? I'm not suggesting that you quit everything, but perhaps your life could use some scaling back.

4. Develop relationships with people who support your endeavors. Spend time with people who encourage you to use your strengths and who make you feel excited about your abilities. This may include people already in your life or might require making new acquaintances. Take a class, volunteer with a cause that interests you or join a group (support group, church etc.) to broaden your social spectrum.

Our strengths are gifts, but if left unused they become like presents under a tree that never get unwrapped. Applying your strengths and values to your life will give you a higher level of satisfaction and happiness, and isn't that a gift we could all use?

Name _____

Address _____ Date _____

R℞ APPLY YOUR VALUES AND LEVERAGE YOUR STRENGTHS

✓ Identify your top values and strengths

✓ Find ways to incorporate what you're good at into your personal and professional life

✓ Reduce activities that don't capitalize on your strengths

✓ Develop relationships with people who encourage you to apply your interests

Signature _____

W: WIN-WINS

FIND WIN-WIN SOLUTIONS IN EVERY SITUATION

> In the Olympics of life, win-win scenarios
> give everyone involved a gold medal.

In his New York Times best-selling book, *The 7 Habits of Highly Effective People*, Dr. Stephen R. Covey highlights the importance of "win-win thinking." Citing it as his fourth most important habit, he says: "Win-win is a frame of mind that constantly seeks mutual benefit in all human interactions. Win-win means that agreements or solutions are mutually beneficial and satisfying."

In short, win-win situations translate into more meaningful relationships, less stress, enhanced productivity and a greater level of overall happiness.

A great example of someone who applies the concept of win-win into her life is Michele Sampson-Smith. After working in television for ten years, Michele decided to pursue her dream: to become an aesthetician.

A single mom, Michele knew she had to generate enough income to support her family, but she also knew she needed to follow what her heart was telling her to do. After considering her options, she left the comforts of her steady job, went back to school for training as an aesthetician and began working at a spa giving facials. The result was a life of pure joy. Michele now loves what she does and the people she works with.

The most amazing part of the story, though, is that Michele prospers almost as much her clients during the facials. "I can't tell you how much I gain from my job. I'm not sure what happens in the treatment room, but there's an exchange that leaves both me and my clients fulfilled. When spirits dance and energies flow, something wonderful and peaceful happens."

Michele finds true happiness comes from providing her services to others, and I guarantee her clients feel the same. "If anyone can find that kind of joy in their work, then they're wealthy, incredibly wealthy - and I'm wealthy in that way. It's definitely a win-win situation."

By following her dream, Michele has brought much happiness into her own life as well as those of her clients. If you're ever in Dallas, Texas, I highly recommend you look her up.[21]

The Diagnosis: Being overly competitive

Competition has been shown to be useful up to a certain point and no further, but co-operation, which is the thing we must strive for today, begins where competition leaves off.

**Franklin D. Roosevelt,
32nd President of the United States**

As the quote above illustrates, competitiveness can be a good thing - especially when we use it to challenge ourselves and grow. Being too competitive, though, can get in the way of finding optimal outcomes for all parties involved.

We live in what can be a dog-eat-dog world, and, sadly, people often stomp on others in their efforts to climb to the top: we compete in work, in relationships and in our homes, and

---

21   *Want a happiness-inducing facial? Visit Michele-Sampson-Smith's website at www.wellnesscarechiro.com and ask for her "Peaceful Experience."*

vie for the best parking spaces, the biggest houses and the most impressive outfits.

When we're overly competitive, we miss out on opportunities to assist those around us and to truly grow ourselves. Collaboration lends itself to happiness not only because we gain something ourselves, but because we're helping others.

Your Prescription: Find balance with win-wins

> *Conflict is inevitable, but combat is optional.*
>
> **-Max Lucado,**
> **Author and Minister**

You can overcome an overly competitive approach with these three, simple tips:

1. Redefine your understanding of winning. Life isn't like the Olympics where only one person can win the gold medal in each event. To enhance happiness, try to redefine "winning" as experiences that benefit everyone involved. In the business world, many companies have found this approach to be beneficial.

Consider the philosophy of Zappos, the online shoe store. They have developed the ultimate win-win in business. CEO Tony Hsieh has said the company's higher purpose is not profit but rather delivering happiness. As a result, much time and money go into enhancing happiness of the employees and their customers.

Regarding employees, for example, the culture is centered on what Hsieh describes as 10 committable core values ("those that we can actually apply"). These include:

- *Create Fun and A Little Weirdness*
- *Be Adventurous, Creative, and Open-Minded*
- *Pursue Growth and Learning*

With respect to this last one, "classic" books like Good to Great *by Jim Collins are available for free to Zappos employees so they can quench their intellectual curiosity and become better people, not to mention workers. Food at the cafeteria and snacks in vending machines are also free to all employees, and cubicles (which even the CEO himself has) are decorated to allow self-expression of fun.*

To make the customer experience as great as possible, when contacting customer service you actually reach a live person, with each representative in the US and trained to be upbeat, kind and helpful. In an effort to make buying shoes on line easy, merchandise can be returned for FREE up to a year after purchase.

The result? A win-win-win. Win for employees, win for customers and win for the company, with gross sales over $1 billion in 2008. Seventy five percent of purchases are made by (happy) repeat customers. And, if you have been to Zappos.com you might notice they sell more than shoes. Why? According to CEO Hsieh because their customers asked for them to sell other items. Seems they want to buy more from this upbeat company.

2. Consciously seek out ways to incorporate win-win situations. As a clinical psychologist and physical therapist, I give lectures around the country. One of my recreational favorite things to do is spending time relaxing at a spa. To put these two things together, I teamed up with Canyon Ranch Resort to coach at their "Thriving with Arthritis" week: I now get to enjoy some R & R while helping people who suffer from chronic pain to better enjoy their lives (one of my passions).

What can you do to incorporate more win-win situations like this in *your* life? Start by figuring out what you like and dislike. When you engage in activities you enjoy, you're more likely to be productive, effective and happy. Conversely, doing what you really don't like can deplete your energy, induce procrastination and sap your positivity.

In his New York Times bestselling book *The Four Hour Workweek*, Tim Ferriss encourages the use of win-win scenarios.

As an example, he recommends outsourcing activities you don't enjoy to others by hiring virtual assistants (VAs). In fact, he attributes a good portion of his wealth and ability to enjoy his life to his use of VAs.

3. Identify how potentially negative situations can become win-wins. Life is filled with little disappointments if we chose to view them that way. Alternatively, we can try to find the "silver lining" when events don't go as we wish. Taking this a step further, we can find positives in selfless acts:

- ✓ Give someone else the "good" parking space so you can benefit from a few extra minutes of exercise with a longer walk
- ✓ Let someone with just a few items get in front of you at the grocery store so you can catch up on the "educational reading" provided near the candy
- ✓ Offer to pick up a friend from the airport: on your way there you can listen to a great story on an audio book, and one the way back you can enjoy hearing about her trip without running up your cellular bill

When you work with others to find joy, your own feelings of satisfaction and happiness get bigger. Do your very best to incorporate more win-win scenarios into your everyday life.

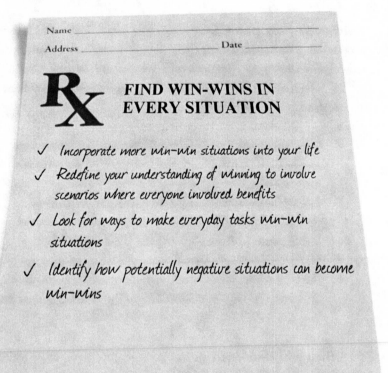

Name _____

Address _____ Date _____

℞ FIND WIN-WINS IN EVERY SITUATION

✓ Incorporate more win-win situations into your life

✓ Redefine your understanding of winning to involve scenarios where everyone involved benefits

✓ Look for ways to make everyday tasks win-win situations

✓ Identify how potentially negative situations can become win-wins

Signature _____

X: eXAMINE YOUR SOUL

USE SPIRITUALITY TO FIND HOPE AND HAPPINESS

> Helpful, healthy and motivating spiritual beliefs
> that you apply in your everyday life are important
> ingredients for a happy life.

Spirituality refers to beliefs about life: its meaning, the purpose of your existence, a sense of who you are and your relationship with something greater than yourself (a higher power, nature etc.).

Spirituality is often simply lumped together with religion. When I ask my clients about their spiritual beliefs, I often hear comments such as, "I'm not very religious" or "I used to go to church when I was younger but don't anymore."

In reality, organized religion is not a necessary component of spirituality, and while not everyone would consider themselves "religious," everyone is spiritual to a greater or lesser degree (whether they realize it or not).

When we have spiritual beliefs that are helpful to us, our satisfaction with life enhances and our joy grows. Take, for example, the Buddhist philosophy[22]. Among other convictions, Buddhists believe that:

---

22   Buddhism is a spiritual belief system that coincides with many formal religions (Christianity, Judaism) but is not itself a religion.

✓ Suffering is a part of life

✓ Wanting (such as wishing others or events to be different) deprives us of contentment and happiness

✓ If we give up unproductive longings and learn to be mindful each day, we can achieve peace and happiness (what Buddhists refer to as "Nirvana")

As a result, those who encompass Buddhist beliefs are less likely to stress out when negative things happen; they're more likely to go with the flow of life's current - accepting and even appreciating whatever life brings. The result? A level of joy and peace both within themselves and between themselves and others.

Buddhism is just one of many examples of spirituality. Regardless of the specifics, when we develop healthy spiritual beliefs and implement them into our everyday lives, we reap some great benefits. These include:

✓ Greater peace
✓ Less depression
✓ A sense of hope
✓ Better physical health
✓ Enhanced happiness

No prescription for true happiness can be complete without a certain level of spiritual awareness and practice.

The Diagnosis: Emptiness from a lack of spirituality

The foundations of a person are not in matter but in spirit.

**-Ralph Waldo Emerson,
Poet and Philosopher**

In today's fast-paced, high-tech world, you may feel overwhelmed just going through your day-to-day activities. So, who has time to ponder their spirituality? I mean, it's not like you're a philosopher.

Determining your view on life and its meaning is important to enhancing your happiness, as it will really boost your joy levels to take your spiritual beliefs seriously. I'm not suggesting you go to a monastery and be silent for six months, but I am recommending that you start to think about how you interpret events that take place - including your purpose here on earth.

Some spiritual beliefs are helpful and empowering: they encourage us to do good deeds and feel good about ourselves. Other spiritual convictions, however, are negative and set us up for unhappiness. Choosing positive beliefs can really improve your life, but choosing negative ones can come to hinder you.

Consider Debbie, who came into see me after her three-year-old son, Aiden, was diagnosed with leukemia. As you can imagine, she was overwhelmingly distraught. This made sense because she was worried about her baby, but as I spoke with her further, it became evident that her spiritual beliefs were contributing to unnecessary stress.

Without being overtly aware of it, Debbie believed that bad things happen because we're being punished for things; she was constantly trying to figure out which of her past wrong-doings was to blame for her son's cancer.

"When I was five, my friends and I threw rocks at a car and we caused an accident," "I dropped out of school when I was seventeen, even though my parents begged me not to," and "I had my baby without being married" were all hypotheses she came up with.

These thoughts caused Debbie a lot of stress, but also hindered her ability to best care for Aiden: she wasn't sleeping, had trouble remembering her son's doctor's appointments and was extremely irritable with the hospital staff.

Together, we examined her spiritual beliefs and how helpful they were being to her. Using this information, Debbie developed more "useful" beliefs such as, "Bad things are just a part of life." As a result, she was able to release her feelings of intense guilt and more effectively cope with her son's diagnosis. With less remorse, she was also able to take care of her own health as well as Aiden's, become less irritable - and even enjoy the time she had with her son during his treatments.

I am happy to tell you that, at the time of this writing, Aiden has been cancer-free for over three years. Debbie continues to apply her helpful spiritual beliefs, too - to which she attributes a great deal of joy and appreciation for her and Aidens' lives.

Your Prescription: Invoke healthy spirituality for a happier life

The purpose of life is to live a life of purpose.

**-Robert Byrne,
World-Renowned Chess Player**

Among other influences, your spiritual beliefs affect how you cope with life's challenges - both major and everyday. To enhance your happiness, develop a belief system that works for you:

1. Determine your own spiritual beliefs. Because spirituality can be a tough subject for some people, the first step to most effectively incorporating it into your life is determining your own beliefs. Doing this may be a difficult process: most people don't know where to start.

You can begin to get an idea of your own spiritual leanings by asking some fundamental questions about life and your role in the universe. Consider, for example:

- ✓ What is your purpose here on earth?
- ✓ Do you believe in a higher power or a connection that ties us all together?
- ✓ Why, in general, do bad things happen? Is it because someone's being punished? Do you see bad things as

random events, or do they have a more positive purpose - such as being learning experiences?

✓ Is there a single destiny or purpose that we are "born" into, or do we create one as we go?

Set some time aside to really think about these questions and take inventory of your spiritual beliefs. Some of these might be more difficult than others to answer: in fact, you might not be able to answer some at all right now. This is okay, as just being aware of their existence is a big step in the right direction.

It may also be helpful to consider one of the above questions, and then just write down anything that comes to mind as a way of answering it.

2. Learn more about different belief systems. Reading about spiritual beliefs can be helpful. The Bible is an important source of spirituality for many, and there are several different versions of it available, such as *The Message*, which have been made easier to understand.

In addition to the Bible, there are countless other books out there, too. Try going to a bookstore and looking under the "Spirituality" section. Two books that I recommend are *When Bad Things Happen to Good People* by Harold S. Kushner and *Awakening Self-Esteem: Spiritual and Psychological Techniques to Enhance Your Well-Being* by Drs. Arthur and Christine Nezu.

Try spending time with others discussing their spirituality as well. To do this, you could attend a church service - or you could just ask friends the questions listed above. This will help you to gain perspective on others' beliefs, and will also let you see which ones "feel" right to you.

3. Find ways to incorporate your spiritual beliefs into your life. A major component of happiness is about not just identifying your spirituality, but also applying it in your everyday life. For example, if you believe in a "Higher Being," prayers of appreciation might be beneficial to you. If your spiritual beliefs include the importance of nature as an extension of yourself, spending time with (and caring for) nature might be one of your priorities.

Steve Harrison was down on his luck. Despite previous successes, including launching the bestselling books Men Are From Mars *and* Chicken Soup for the Soul, *the company he and his brother, Bill, owned was at risk of going bankrupt. They had invested significant funds into the company for long-term gain, but had little revenue for the immediate future. Even now he tears up just thinking about what he then feared was inevitable: closing his publicity business and laying off employees who were like family to him and his brother.*

A devout Christian, Steve has a strong belief that difficult times are meant to shape you so you can help others. He had faith that this was a calling card to change his strategy - to be more creative in his approach.

"I kept thinking of the story where Jesus and the Disciples are fishing all night and they haven't caught anything. Then Jesus says, 'Put your net on the other side of the boat.' When they do this, they get so many fish that their nets almost burst."

Keeping in mind his spiritual beliefs, Steve came up with an idea. He was about to give a talk to a group about services his company offered: a speech he had given many times before, often without drumming up much business. This time, he made a tweak ("I put my net on the other side") and decided to offer a payment plan. This would allow the audience to purchase services that would benefit their companies at a cost they could afford. Because of this one idea, Steve generated over $65,000 in single day.

Today, Steve and Bill's company, FreePublicity.com, is thriving to say the least.[23] *By continuing to apply his spiritual beliefs, they're*

---

23   For more information on Steve and Bill's company, visit their website at www.freepublicity.com.

now generating over $4 million annual revenue - and no one has had to be laid off.

What's more, Steve enjoys true happiness: not just because of his financial comforts, but because he incorporates his spirituality into his everyday life.

Try it today: focus on identifying ways to implement your spiritual beliefs, and then take note of the impact this single step has on your happiness levels. I think you'll be impressed.

Name _____

Address _____ Date _____

R̽ EXAMINE YOUR SOUL

✓ Incorporate your spiritual beliefs into your everyday life

✓ Identify your own spiritual ideals

✓ Learn more about others' spirituality to see what "feels right" to you

✓ Find ways to apply your spiritual beliefs

Signature _____

Y: *YOU TIME*

PRIORITIZE TIME TO TAKE CARE OF YOU

> Put your oxygen mask on first. You're no good
> to anyone if you're not breathing.

Devoting quality time to yourself is an essential part of any quest for happiness. Despite the demands of the world, it's important to establish time to addressing your needs and wants. "You time" can be spent by yourself or with others, but it needs to be targeted on bringing greater joy into your life.

Many people struggle to justify dedicating any of their precious time to themselves, as they fear it is a sign of being selfish. In reality, having a moderate amount of time to yourself will not make you egocentric, but *will* make you more relaxed, more appreciative, better able to help others, and yes – you guessed it – happier!

Focusing on people aside from yourself is crucial too, of course, and many chapters in this book focus on how to make the most of doing just that. Compassion and quality time, however, aren't just reserved for other people: you deserve these gifts as well.

As we explore the importance of "you time," remember that the key is *quality*, not quantity. Spending eight hours in front of the television will do little to make you happier, but an hour devoted to your mind and body's wellness may just do the trick.

The Diagnosis: Self neglect

Declare today "sacred time"- off-limits to everyone, unless invited by you. Take care of your personal wants and needs. Say no, graciously but firmly, to others' demands.

**-Oprah Winfrey,
Media Icon**

Some of you might be scoffing at the idea of time for yourself and wondering, "Is she crazy? Does she have any idea how much I have to do already? There's no time for me!" This reaction is common, but understand that if having some quality time to yourself seems like an unattainable luxury, you need "you time" more than you realize!

Consider what type of person you are when you're feeling overwhelmed, overworked or otherwise stressed out: how pleasant, productive and positive are you? Probably not very - I know from both professional and personal experiences that that's almost certainly true. Most of us are happier when we have some time to ourselves to decompress and relax.

Repeat this mantra: "In order to be a good **X** (worker, wife, mother, friend etc.), I need to take care of myself." Again, this doesn't mean to *only* think of yourself, but it does mean that it's important to take some time to refresh and revive.

For Anne Jolles and her husband, Jon, it seemed like a typical Fourth of July: they'd spent the day with family and had just decided to sneak away together to watch the fireworks. Within minutes, however, Jon went from feeling fine to having difficulty breathing. Anne called 911 and her husband was rushed to the hospital.

The Jolles family eventually learned that Jon had a tumor on his kidney, which was a rare form of adrenal cancer. They were told that the tumor itself was extremely dangerous while still in his body AND that the surgery to remove it had some major risks. Doctors recommended that they get their affairs in order before the operation . . .

Needless to say, this was an incredibly stressful time for the entire family. Amidst all of these worries with Jon in the hospital for weeks, Anne had to support her children emotionally and maintain her busy life-coaching business.[24] There were a lot of people who were counting on her, but she realized she needed to be able to count on herself, too.

Every day, while Jon was in the hospital, she spent her mornings at home with her children. She would then go to the hospital to be with her husband - often staying past dinner. When she got home, she grabbed the only time left to dedicate to herself: "you time."

Taking advantage of the long summer days, Anne and her next-door neighbor went biking every evening. Sometimes they went for half an hour, sometimes for an hour and a half – calling themselves the "Nightriders" because of how they'd often ride in the dark.

During these bike rides, Anne could process her day: "It was a fabulous outlet with such an amazing sense of camaraderie and support. There was no judgment; my friend just listened and encouraged me. I was exercising - out in nature and under the cover of darkness. It felt so private. All of that really helped me cope with my emotions and my anxiety. It was almost like being let out of jail, I felt so free." Anne attributes her resilience during such a difficult period to taking this "you time" for herself.

Happily, Jon recovered from his severe illness and now has a great prognosis. The "Nightriders" continue on their nightly excursions, too, but now with one more: Jon has joined the group. They all enjoy the physical and psychological benefits of "you time."

Your Prescription: Find more "you time"

In case of emergency, put your own oxygen mask on first before assisting others.

-Advice from Airlines

---

24   *For more information on Anne Jolles, her coaching and her books, visit her website at www.annejolles.com.*

The airlines have it right: you can't be at your best to help out others if you haven't first helped yourself. Devoting time to "you" is critical.

Understanding the inherent challenges that present themselves while trying to find more "you time," I've put together the following steps to help simplify things:

1. Identify and prioritize how you spend your time. Sit down and document how you spend your day. This will probably include things like taking care of your family, working, driving in the car, paying bills, cleaning your home, talking to neighbors you might not even like and performing activities that you don't necessarily enjoy. You will probably be surprised to see how you really spend your time.

Now, how can you realistically get rid of unnecessary or happiness-depleting tasks to incorporate more "you time"? As an example, consider that the average American watches almost five hours of TV each day. What could you do with that time (or even just *some* of that time) to really focus on your happiness?

2. Simplify your life. Our lives tend to be complicated and hectic, which doesn't make for a good happiness prescription.

Try taking these steps to help simplify things and clean out your schedule for more "you time":

- ✓ **Disconnect from information overload.** Have set times (only once or twice a day) to check your email, voicemail, social media sites and stick to these rigidly. If you're concerned that others will have a hard time with you doing this, include a message about the times you check your messages and what someone can do to get immediate assistance (call someone else, visit a website etc.).
- ✓ **Organize yourself.** Ever feel stressed out because you can't find something or have too much clutter? Organizing yourself and your life can help

tremendously. You can certainly do this yourself, but there are also websites, books and coaches who can really to help you to get better sorted.[25]

✓ **Learn how to implement a life of simplicity.** There's a great free resource developed by Mark Joyner called "Simpleology" that takes you through a series of twelve steps to simplify your life. Touted as the "simple science of getting what you want," this course really teaches you how to keep focused on what's important to you - and to let go of the other stuff that's getting in the way of your happiness.

3. Take a time out. Schedule and protect your "you time" as you would an important meeting. You wouldn't miss one of these, so why would you miss time for yourself? If it helps, try to have different activities in mind for the different amount of times you manage to catch:

5-10 minutes: Meditate, review your positive goals for the day, go for a stroll around the block, stretch, enjoy a cup of coffee, pray or take a warm shower.

20 minutes: Write in your journal, read, perform a relaxation exercise, take a bubble bath, go for a jog with a friend or enjoy a power nap.

Over the week: Take a class, be a tourist in your own town, have a fun lunch with a friend or go on an afternoon date with yourself.

Over the month: Indulge in a massage or facial, go for a long hike, cook a glorious meal or read a book about a subject important to you.

---

25   One of my favorite places to learn about better organization is Patty Kreamer's site, www.byebyeclutter.com.

4. Say NO. You don't have to do everything, and you *can* back out of obligations that cause you excessive stress. As we discussed in *Chapter* T: *Talking*, being assertive entails standing up for yourself while still being respectful to others.

If you can learn to say "no" to some requests so that you can take care of yourself, in the long run you *and* those around you will be happier.

Devoting time to yourself will give you more energy, greater happiness and a sense of rejuvenation to take on the challenges that life presents. Go ahead, give yourself the gift of "you time." You deserve it.

Name _____

Address _____ Date _____

 **FIND TIME FOR YOU**

✓ Identify and prioritize time for yourself

✓ Simplify your life by disconnecting from the overload of information, organizing yourself and keeping yourself focused on what's important

✓ Take time out for yourself

✓ Learn to say no to demands that you don't have time to fulfill

Signature _____

Z: ZZZ

GET YOUR SLEEP

> Sleep is an invaluable but often underappreciated commodity: if experienced in proper amounts, it can positively influence your health, happiness, relationships, bank account - and even your waistline.

Ever have trouble falling or staying asleep? If so, you're not alone: sixty million Americans suffer from sleep disturbance at some point in their lives.

Lack of sleep has real effects on our mental and physical health - including increased stress levels, depression, anxiety, low energy, pain, shortness of temper and reduced effectiveness. Sometimes its symptoms can even be similar to those commonly associated with attention deficit hyperactivity disorder (ADHD).

Weight gain is another thing reduced "zzzs" can contribute to. In a study with over sixty-eight-thousand women, it was found that those women who slept five hours or less per night were almost a third more likely to gain thirty pounds or more over a sixteen year period (as compared with women who slept seven hours per night). This weight gain was unrelated to diet or physical activity. I doubt that the increased pounds made these tired women too happy, either.

Not only does sleeplessness take a toll on your own health, but it also taxes society: medical expenses and loss of productivity at work associated with insomnia are estimated to cost about $100 billion annually. Imagine how much better the world would run if everyone had a good night's sleep!

The Diagnosis: Sleep walking through the day

> *No day is so bad it can't be fixed with a nap.*
>
> **-Carrie Snow,**
> **Stand-up Comedian**

Without enough sleep, we become easily worn out and our ability to maintain a happy, fulfilling lifestyle becomes severely limited.

How are you doing with your sleep? Do you:

✓ Get at least eight hours most nights?
✓ Sleep through the night without waking up?
✓ Wake up feeling refreshed and excited about beginning the day?
✓ Feel relaxed in bed?

If you answered "no" to any of these questions, addressing your sleep may be an important part of your happiness prescription.

When Kate came in to see me, she was a self-proclaimed "mess." Her job in sales was extremely demanding and required her to travel three days out of each week, but having trouble sleeping in hotels, she would often lie awake for hours worrying that her inevitable fatigue would lead to failed sales. This, of course, inflated her stress levels even more - perpetuating her sleeplessness.

Eventually, she decided to find something to help her. She first considered trying to get a prescription from her doctor, but was fearful it would become addictive. As a solution, she decided to have a few glasses of wine each night when she was on the road. The alcohol was good at getting her to fall asleep initially (and often quite quickly), but by two or three o'clock in the morning she was awake and unable to return to her slumber.

Next, she decided to try an over-the-counter sleeping aid, and took one every night for a year before she came to see me. As reasoning, she said, "I have to. Otherwise, there's no way I can sleep, and if I don't sleep, I'm useless."

With this method, she generally got around six hours of sleep per night, but had very low energy levels throughout the day. "I'm exhausted. I have to pump myself full of coffee all day just to stay somewhat alert. I'm crabby with my husband because I feel so drained. We haven't been intimate for I don't even know how long because I'm just too tired. All I want to do when I get home from work is sleep."

Using the solutions outlined below, we worked together to get her off the pills and caffeine. For the first time, she was now finding her sleep restorative. Her productivity sky-rocketed as a result, and by the time we'd finished working together she'd landed a hugely competitive account that she'd been too stretched to even pitch. "I felt so much more confident and able to think on my feet; my presentations have never been this good," she said, attributing the account win to her improved sleep.

In addition to benefits at work, Kate's home life also dramatically improved, and the previously strained relationship with her husband recovered as her stress levels and exhaustion decreased. "I'm not short-tempered with him all the time like I used to be. We have fun again, like when we first got married. I like spending time with him and feel closer when we're together."

So, what about you? Do you think that you, like Kate, could improve aspects of your life by getting better sleep? You might be surprised at how powerful this part of the happiness prescription can be.

Your Prescription: Find your "zzzs"

> *A good laugh and a long sleep are the best*
> *cures in the doctor's book.*
> **-Irish Proverb**

You might be wondering: "Can't I just take a pill if I have trouble sleeping?" The answer, of course, is yes, but medications can be habit-forming and may cause sluggishness the next day as we saw with Kate.

Also, behavioral solutions such as those presented below have been proven to be *more* helpful than sleeping pills in the long run - without any of the adverse side effects. Try them tonight to get a better night's sleep:

1. Prioritize sleep and optimize sleeping conditions. Get to sleep at a decent hour. Turn off the TV, computer and cell phone so they don't disturb you. Make your bedroom sleep friendly, too, by providing comforts such as soft bedding and thick curtains.

2. Follow a wind-down routine to help you relax before bedtime. Take a warm shower, listen to relaxing music with the lights dimmed, meditate or read. Relaxing the body and mind before getting into bed can also help decrease stress and stressful thoughts.

3. Keep your thoughts in check. Thoughts such as "I have to get sleep tonight or I won't be able to function tomorrow . . ." will only stress you out. Do something to relax and distract your mind such as saying to yourself, "I allow my mind and body to relax."

For some, keeping a journal next to their bed is helpful. In it, they can write down what's on their mind before bed, or if they wake up in the middle of the night with an idea, they jot it down and then go back to sleep. This helps to keep the thoughts out of their head when it's not a convenient time to think about them.

4. Watch what you eat and drink close to your bedtime. Caffeine, nicotine and alcohol all deter a good sleep, so try to keep the first two (if necessary) to hours before five o'clock p.m.

Alcohol may help you fall asleep, but can severely inhibit restful and consistent sleep; try a warm bath or relaxation CD prior to bed instead of an alcoholic drink.

5. Remember that *everyone* has difficulty sleeping at some point. Just because you have difficulty at one time doesn't mean it'll last through the night or continue for the entire week. However, if your insomnia persists for more than two or three weeks, contact your doctor for advice.

A good night's sleep will help enhance your happiness. Give it a try tonight!

Name _____

Address _____ Date _____

℞ MAKE SLEEP A TOP PRIORITY

✓ Prioritize sleep

✓ Optimize sleeping conditions

✓ Establish a regular routine to wind down before bed

✓ Keep your thoughts in check

✓ Watch what you eat and drink near bedtime

✓ Don't worry about the occasional restless night – everyone has difficulty sleeping sometimes

Signature _____

YOUR ULTIMATE HAPPINESS Rx

Thousands of candles can be lit from a single candle, and the life of the candle will not be shortened. Happiness never decreases by being shared.

-Buddha

The last twenty-six chapters have showed you *many* ways for making your lifestyle healthier and happier. If you put them into practice, you'll experience new levels of joy and satisfaction – levels you might never before have thought possible! In addition, the more you use the techniques, the more effective they will become!

To get the most out of your happiness prescription, feel free to start anywhere you like: just open the book at a page and begin there, or scan through it to find something which "speaks" to you.

When you've decided on what "medication" you want to take, be sure to remember that change can sometimes be difficult – even if you know you want it. If you're having problems, don't worry – just give yourself a break, figure out why your old habits are back, and then work out what you can do better next time. Keep at it, and the rewards will come to you in no time.

To further boost your success, why not take the **happiness challenge?**

Take the Happiness Challenge

Taking the happiness challenge is a great way of condensing down all of this book's messages into five simple steps. It's not a supplement for reading each chapter, but it will let you see great results quickly if you stick to it – so why not give it a go?

Step 1 – Identify something that often makes you unhappy. This could be being stuck in traffic, seeing your child's room always messy, getting stress from work or anything similar: it just has to lower your mood and happen on a regular basis.

Step 2 – Write down three positive ways of looking at the situation. Once you've come up with a situation you don't like, find three ways of seeing it in a positive light and write them down. If you're struggling to uncover your problem's silver lining, there are plenty of hints given throughout this book which should help you out – but here are few common examples to get you started:

Current challenge	Positive perspective
Rush hour traffic	"I 'm grateful to have a car."
Child's room is a mess	"I'm so lucky to have a child at all – this is only a tiny problem."
Long line at the store	"I'm in this store because I've got enough money to buy things."
Too much work	"I have a job and I can rely on my colleagues if this really gets to be too much."
Plane flight cancelled because of bad weather	"I'm happy to be safe on the ground rather than bouncing around in the plane with this storm."
I have a million things to do on my to-do list and can't get them all done	"I'm so fortunate that I have the ability to help so many people - including myself."

Step 3 – Read the list out loud regularly. Now you have identified three ways of seeing the problem positively. Every morning and night, read the three positive aspects out loud to yourself several times. This will keep them in your mind, and gradually begin to make you think more optimistically about the original problem.

Step 4 – Stop any negative thoughts. If you ever start to feel down about the situation, do something to snap yourself out of the funk. This could be twenty jumping jacks, singing a "feel good" song or just changing your watch over to the opposite wrist – anything that prompts your body and mind to see the situation from a different perspective. Then read over your list from above.

Step 5 – Repeat for a month. The best way to really change your opinion on a common problem is to keep this routine up for an extended period. Do all the steps above every day for a month and you'll be sure to have a very different outlook by the end.

When you're done, visit www.ahappyyou.com and let me (and the world!) know about your experiences with the challenge. Many stories are featured there from people who have excelled at the happiness challenge, so it's a great place to go for both encouragement and to share your successes.

Share the Wealth

I really urge you to take the **happiness challenge**, but I also strongly hope you'll share what you've learned in this book with others. Let's spread happiness around the world!

Sometimes I imagine a "Happiness Movement" like the one for the environment. A couple of decades ago, global warming was a new thing to most people, but now everyone knows what it is: why can't we do the same for personal satisfaction?

Whenever you get the chance, spread the great news. As well as improving your own life, take the time to tell friends, family, co-workers and even strangers about how to be happier and how to reduce their stress levels regardless of their circumstances. Encourage them to take the happiness challenge, too!

This is especially effective when you bump into people who radiate negativity. I'm sure you know who I mean: the disgruntled shopper causing a problem for a sales assistant, a neighbor who makes it her job to point out all the bad things in life, a co-worker who constantly complains, etc. If you've ever been tempted to tell them to "Chill out!" or "Give me a break!" before, now you've got a reason to!

Start by offering them a "Take the Happiness Challenge!" card:

These are available from www.ahappyyou.com and don't cost you anything except for a small shipping and handling fee. They explain the general concepts of the happiness prescription and give some useful tips on how to change negativity into positive energy. They're a great way of reminding yourself of the principles - as well as helping others start their journey.

Regardless of what's going on in your life, you can be happy if you believe in your inner ability to make positive changes. All you have to do is stick to your Rx and wait to feel yourself come alive!

Don't wait another moment – start your happiness prescription now!

END NOTES

Page xiv: "*Happiness depends...*" Inspirational-Quotes.info, *Happiness Quotes*, www.inspirational-quotes.info/happiness. html (Jun. 22, 2009).

Page xvi "*The message is the medicine*"... *Oprah.com,* Dr. Oz on Multiple Orgasms, *www.oprah.com/article/ oprahshow/20090423-tows-best-dr-oz/5 (Jun. 22, 2009).*

Page xx "*Nothing can bring you...*" ThinkExist.com, *Ralph Waldo Emerson Quotes*, www.thinkexist.com/quotation/ nothing_can_bring_you_happiness_but_yourself/14510. html (Jun. 22, 2009).

Page 2 "*I had the blues...*" Dale Carnegie, *How to Enjoy Your Life and Your Job: Selections from How to Win Friends and Influence People and How to Stop Worrying and Start Living* (New York: Simon and Schuster, 1990), 47.

Page 4 "*If you don't think...*" ThinkExist.com, *Cavett Robert Quotes*, www.thinkexist.com/quotation/if_you_don-t_ think_every_day_is_a_good_day-just/201079.html (Jun. 22, 2009).

Page 5 *What Christopher Reeve missed...* ThinkExist.com, *Christopher Reeve Quotes*, www.thinkexist.com/quotation/ the-thing-that-i-want-more-though-is-to-be-able/606147. html (Jun. 22, 2009).

Page 6 *"It's not having…"* Sheryl Crow, *Soak Up The Sun*, Album: *C'MON C'MON*, (A&M Records, 2002).

Page 8 *"It's a simple message…"* Blackcatter's World of TV Theme Song Lyrics, *Arthur and Friends*, www.cfhf.net/lyrics/arthur.htm (Jun. 22, 2009).

Page 9 *"In a decisive set…"* ThinkExist.com, *Chris Evert Quotes*, www.thinkexist.com/quotation/you-ve_got_to_take_the_initiative_and_play_your/151143.html (Jun. 22, 2009).

Page 9 *Colonel Sanders…* John Pearce, *The Colonel* (New York: Doubleday, 1982),

Page 9 *Person of the Century…* Time Magazine, *Person of the Century* (Jan. 3, 2000).

Page 10 *"A man cannot…"* The Quotations Page, *Quote Details: Mark Twain*, www.quotationspage.com/quote/2156.html (Jun. 22, 2009).

Page 11 *Hilary Swank…* Academy of Achievement, *Hilary Swank Biography*, www.achievement.org/autodoc/page/swa0bio-1 (Jun. 22, 2009).

Page 11 *"Self confidence…"* The Quotations Page, *Quote Details: Samuel Johnson*, www.quotationspage.com/quote/1511.html (Jun. 22, 2009).

Page 15 *"Nothing is impossible…"* Olympics: ESPN, *Mission accomplished: Phelps earns eighth gold in medley relay,* www.sports.espn.go.com/oly/summer08/swimming/news/story?id=3538984 (Jun. 22, 2009).

Page 16 *"A typical day…"* Mihaly Csikszentmihalyi, *Finding Flow: The Psychology of Engagement with Everyday Life* (New York: BasicBooks, 1997).

Page 16 *"If at first..."* ThinkExist.com, *Albert Einstein Quotes* www.thinkexist.com/quotation/if_at_first-the_idea_is_not_absurd-then_there_is/180160.html (Jun. 22, 2009).

Page 16 *Creative people...* Steven Pritzker and Mark Runco, *Encyclopedia of Creativity Set* (New York: Academic Press, 1999).

Page 18 "Happiness is not..." WisdomQuotes.com, Happiness Quotes, *www.wisdomquotes.com/cat_happiness.html (Jun. 22, 2009).*

Page 19 *Peter Shankman...* Peter Schankman, *Can We Do That?! Outrageous PR Stunts That Work - And Why Your Company Needs Them* (New York: Wiley, 2006).

Page 21 *John Maclean...* John Maclean, *Sucking the Marrow Out of Life: The John MacLean Story* (Sydney: Murdoch Books, 2005).

Page 23 *"My definition of success..."* QuotationsBook, *Robbins, Anthony Quote,* www.quotationsbook.com/quote/37747/ (Jun. 22, 2009).

Page 24 *"To freely bloom..."* Gerry Spence, *How to Argue and Win Every Time* (New York: St. Martin's Griffin, 1996).

Page 29 *Joanne Giannini...* Prevention.com, *"I'm So Confident Now!",* www.prevention.com/cda/article/i-m-so-confident-now/0a0657446c187110VgnVCM10000013281eac____/ weight.loss/success.stories/0/0/0/1 (Jun. 22, 2009).

Page 30 *Physical health...* MayoClinic.com, *Exercise: 7 benefits of regular physical activity,* www.mayoclinic.com/health/ exercise/HQ01676%20&%20 (Jun. 22, 2009).

Page 30 *"Those who think..."* The Quote Garden, *Exercise Quotes,* www.quotegarden.com/exercise.html (Jun. 22, 2009).

Page 30 *Exercise & depression study...* James Blumenthal Michael Babyak, Steve Herman, Parinda Khatri, Murali Doraiswamy, Kathleen Moore, Edward Craighead, Teri Baldewicz and Ranga Krishnan, *Exercise Treatment for Major Depression: Maintenance of Therapeutic Benefit at 10 Months* (Psychosomatic Medicine, 2000), 62: 633-638.

Page 31 *"The perils of overwork..."* ThinkExist.com, *Thomas Alva Edison Quotes*, www.thinkexist.com/quotation/the_ perils_of_overwork_are_slight_compared_with/177385. html (Jun. 22, 2009).

Page 31 *CDC stats...* Centers for Disease Control and Prevention, *Physical Activity Statistics: Introduction*, www.cdc. gov/nccdphp/dnpa/physical/stats/index.htm (Jun. 22, 2009).

Page 31 *"The reason I exercise..."* BrainyQuote.com, *Kenneth H. Cooper Quotes*, www.brainyquote.com/quotes/quotes/k/ kennethhc357497.html (Jun. 22, 2009).

Page 35 *The Dancer...* Susan Titus, *The Dancer Returns* (iUniverse, Inc., 2007).

Page 36 *"To forgive is..."* ThinkExist.com, *Lewis B. Smedes Quotes*, www.thinkexist.com/quotation/to_forgive_is_to_ set_a_prisoner_free_and_discover/214491.html (Jun. 22, 2009).

Page 37 *Forgiveness...* Amsa.org, *Healing Through Forgiveness*, www.amsa.org/healingthehealer/forgiveness.cfm (Jun. 22, 2009).

Page 38 *Dong Yun Yoon...* CNN, *Story about Dong Yun Yoon and coverage of his press conference* (Dec. 10, 2008).

Page 39 *"To forgive is..."* ThinkExist.com, *Robert Muller Quotes*, www.thinkexist.com/quotation/to-forgive-is-the-highest- most-beautiful-form-of/390790.html (Jun. 22, 2009).

Page 44 *"If you want…"* ThinkExist.com, *Albert Einstein Quotes*, www.thinkexist.com/quotation/if_you_want_to_live_a_happy_life-tie_it_to_a_goal/145945.html (Jun. 22, 2009).

Page 46 *"Without goals…"* ThinkExist.com, *Fitzhugh Dodson Quotes*, www.thinkexist.com/quotation/without_goals-and_plans_to_reach_them-you_are/252600.html (Jun. 22, 2009).

Page 47 *"I'm not discouraged…"* ThinkExist.com, *Thomas Alva Edison Quotes* www.thinkexist.com/quotation/i_am_not_discouraged-because_every_wrong_attempt/14881.html (Jun. 22, 2009).

Page 47 *Three Cups of Tea…* Greg Mortenson and David Relin, *Three Cups of Tea: One Man's Mission to Promote Peace . . . One School at a Time* (New York: Penguin, 2007).

Page 49 *"Sometimes…"* ThinkExist.com, *Charles M. Schulz Quotes*, www.en.thinkexist.com/quotation/sometimes_i_lie_awake_at_night-and_ask--where/8737.html (Jun. 22, 2009).

Page 50 *Benefits of humor…* Helpguide.org, *Understand, Prevent and Resolve Life's Challenges*, www.helpguide.org (Jun. 22, 2009).

Page 50 *"If at first…"* Weather.net, *Steve Wright Quotes*, www.weather.net/zarg/ZarPages/stevenWright.html (Jun. 22, 2009).

Page 51 *Tina Fey…* ThinkExist.com, *Tina Fey Quotes*, www.en.thinkexist.com/quotation/maternity-leave-is-over-for-tina-fey-of-saturday/633663.html (Jun. 22, 2009).

Page 51 *Dane Cook…* Logan.ws, *Dane Cook Quotes*, www.logan.ws/quotes/danecook.asp (Jun. 22, 2009).

Page 51 *Steve Martin…* ThinkExist.com, *Steve Martin Quotes*, www.en.thinkexist.com/quotation/first_the_doctor_told_me_the_good_news-i_was/220018.html (Jun. 22, 2009).

Page 51 *Robin Williams...* ThinkExist.com, *Robin Williams Quotes*, www.en.thinkexist.com/quotation/if_it-s_the_psychic_network_why_do_they_need_a/223913.html (Jun. 22, 2009).

Page 51 *"Celebrate..."* FreshThinkingBusiness.com, *Sam Walton: 10 Rules for Building a Successful Business*, www.freshthinkingbusiness.com/walton-business-rules.html (Jun. 22, 2009).

Page 51 *"Don't sweat..."* ThinkExist.com, *George Carlin Quotes*, www.thinkexist.com/quotation/don-t_sweat_the_petty_things_and_don-t_pet_the/160607.html (Jun. 22, 2009).

Page 52 *"I'm not..."* ThinkExist.com, *Quotes*, www.thinkexist.com/quotation/i-m_not_a_complete_idiot-some_parts_are/187018.html (Jun. 22, 2009).

Page 53 *"They told me..."* Emily Pettigrew - St. James Encyclopedia of Pop Culture, *Ellen DeGeneres* www.findarticles.com/p/articles/mi_g1epc/is_bio/ai_2419200297 (Jun. 22, 2009).

Page 59 *King Arthur...* Monty Python and the Holy Grail, *(Twentieth Century Fox, 1975)*.

Page 59 *"Jut don't..."* QuotationsBook.com, *Ella Fitzgerald Quotes* www.quotationsbook.com/quote/13721 (Jun. 22, 2009).

Page 61 *"If your actions..."* WisdomQuotes.com, *Leadership Quotes*, www.wisdomquotes.com/cat_leadership.html (Jun. 22, 2009).

Page 62 *Drew Carey...* NBC Access Hollywood, *Interview with Nancy O'Dell* (2007).

Page 62 *J.K. Rowling...* From an interview with Adeel Amini for a student magazine at Edinburgh University.

Page 62 *Billy Joel...* Billy Joel, *The Official Billy Joel Site*, www.billyjoel.com (Jun. 22, 2009).

Page 66 *"Journal writing..."* KiTT.NeT, *Journal Writing is a Voyage to . . .* www.quote.kitt.net/2009/01/journal-writing-is-voyage-to.html (Jun. 22, 2009).

Page 67 *Dr. James Pennebaker...* James Pennbaker, *Emotion, Disclosure & Health* (Washington DC: American Psychological Association, 2002).

Page 68 *"I never travel..."* About.com Classic Literature, *The Importance of Being Earnest Quotes,* www.classiclit.about.com/od/importanceofbeingearnest/a/aa_impearnquote.htm (Jun. 22, 2009).

Page 71 *Michael Oher...* Michael Lewis, *The Blind Side: Evolution of a Game* (New York: W.W.Norton & Co., 2006).

Page 71 Michael Oher... CBS CSTV, A Diamond in the Rough, www.youtube.com/watch?v=9FhlbsJUJ9Q (2008).

Page 72 *Volunteering...* Corporation for National and Community Service, *The Health Benefits of Volunteering: A Review of Recent Research,* www.nationalservice.gov/pdf/07_0506_hbr.pdf (Jun. 22, 2009).

Page 73 *"We make a ..."* QuotationsPage.com, *Winston Churchill Quotes,* www.quotationspage.com/quote/2236.html (Jun. 22, 2009).

Page 74 *"Kindness is..."* ThinkExist.com, *Mark Twain Quotes,* www.en.thinkexist.com/quotation/kindness_is_a_language_which_the_deaf_can_hear/14177.html (Jun. 22, 2009).

Page 76 *"I'm a big believer…"* ThinkExist.com, *Nancy Reagan Quotes*, www.en.thinkexist.com/quotation/i_am_a_big_believer_that_eventually_everything/217115.html (Jun. 22, 2009).

Page 77 *Susan G Komen…* Nancy Brinker, *Winning the Race: Taking Charge of Breast Cancer* (Tapestry Press, 2001).

Page 78 *Social support…* PsychCentral.com, *Physiological Benefits from Social Support*, www.psychcentral.com/news/2008/09/19/physiological-benefits-from-social-support/2970.html (Jun. 22, 2009).

Page 78 *"Shower the people…"* James Taylor, Album: *Greatest Hits*, (Rhino/Wea, Los Angeles, 1976).

Page 79 *Cari Shane Parven…* Molly Rosen, *Knowing Pains: Women on Love, Sex and Work in Our 40s* (Livermore, CA: WingSpan Press, 2008).

Page 79 "Shared joy…" ThinkExist.com, Swedish Proverb Quotes, www.thinkexist.com/quotation/shared_joy_is_a_double_joy-shared_sorrow_is_half/176839.html (Jun. 22, 2009).

Page 84 *Mindfulness…* Victoria Follette and Marsha Linehan Stephen Hayes, *Mindfulness and Acceptance: Expanding the Cognitive-Behavioral Tradition* (New York: The Guilford Press, 2004).

Page 85 *"Pick the day…"* QuotesAndPoems.com, *Audrey Hepburn Quotes*, www.quotesandpoem.com/quotes/showquotes/author/audrey-hepburn/126626 (Jun. 22, 2009).

Page 86 *"The most precious…"* ThinkExist.com, *Mindfulness Quotes*, www.thinkexist.com/quotes/with/keyword/mindfulness/ (Jun. 22, 2009).

Page 92 *"He that takes…"* The Quote Garden, *Ayurveda Quotes*
www.quotegarden.com/ayurveda.html (Jun. 22, 2009).

Page 93 *Diet & depression…* American Dietetic Association,
Homepage, www.eatright.org/cps/rde/xchg/ada/hs.xsl/index.
html (Jun. 22, 2009).

Page 93 *"It's difficult…"* ThinkExist.com, *Lewis Grizzard Quotes*,
www.thinkexist.com/quotation/it-s_difficult_to_think_
anything_but_pleasant/340292.html (Jun. 22, 2009).

Page 94 *"I was raised…"* EvanCarmichael.com, *Rachael Ray Quotes*,
www.evancarmichael.com/Famous-Entrepreneurs/1506/
Rachael-Ray-Quotes.html (Jun. 22, 2009).

Page 95 *GoChi…* Harunobu Amagase and Dwight Nance, *A
Randomized, Double-Blind, Placebo-Controlled, Clinical
Study of the General Effects of a Standardized Lycium
barbarum (Goji) Juice, GoChi™* (The Journal of Alternative
and Complementary Medicine, 2008), 14(4): 403-412.

Page 96 *Fat in your diet…* Nicholas Read, Anita Wells, Jonathan
Laugharne and N.S. Ahluwalia, *Alterations in Mood After
Changing to a Low-Fat Diet* (British Journal of Nutrition,
1998), 79(1):23-30. .

Page 100 *Optimists versus pessimists…* Martin Seligman,
Learned Optimism: How to Change Your Mind and Your Life
(London: Vintage, 2006).

Page 100 *"Everyone thought…"* CNN, *Article on and interview
with Earvin "Magic" Johnson* (Jun. 22, 2005).

Page 101 *"A pessimist…"* ThinkExist.com, *Optimism Quotes*,
www.thinkexist.com/quotations/optimism (Jun. 22, 2009).

Page 103 *"When one door…"* QuoteWorld.org, *Alexander Bell
Quotes*, www.quoteworld.org/quotes/1168 (Jun. 22, 2009).

Page 104 *"Don't cry..."* ThinkExist.com, *Dr. Seuess Quotes*, www.thinkexist.com/quotes/dr._seuss (Jun. 22, 2009).

Page 104 *"A home..."* Ghar Sita Mutu, *House With A Heart*, www.gharsitamutu.com (Jun. 22, 2009).

Page 108 *Problem solving benefits...* Arthur and Christine Nezu and Tom D'Zurilla, *Solving Life's Problems: A 5-Step Guide to Enhanced Well-Being* (New York: Springer Publishing Company, 2006).

Page 108 *"No problem..."* ThinkExist.com, *Voltaire Quotes*, www.thinkexist.com/quotation/no_problem_can_withstand_the_assault_of_sustained/259986.html (Jun. 22, 2009).

Page 109 *"All the world..."* QuotationsPage.com, *Helen Keller Quotes*, www.quotationspage.com/quote/1632.html (Jun. 22, 2009).

Page 112 *"A bend..."* The Quote Garden, *Hang in There Quotes*, www.quotegarden.com/hang-in.html (Jun. 22, 2009).

Page 115 *"If you don't..."* ThinkExist.com, *Maya Angelou Quotes*, www.thinkexist.com/quotation/if_you_don-t_like_something-change_it-if_you_can/148684.html (Jun. 22, 2009).

Page 116 *"No man..."* QuotationsPage.com, *Publilius Syrus Quotes,* www.quotationspage.com/quote/24393.html (Jun. 22, 2009).

Page 117 *Every Child, Inc...* EveryChildInc.org, *Every Child Inc. Homepage*, www.everychildinc.org (Jun. 22, 2009).

Page 124 *Relaxation effects...* MayoClinic.com, *Relaxation techniques: Learn ways to reduce your stress*, www.mayoclinic.com/health/relaxation-technique/SR00007 (Jun. 22, 2009).

Page 125 *"For fast-acting..."* LilyTomlin.com, *Lily Quotes*, www.lilytomlin.com/lily/quotes.htm (Jun. 22, 2009).

Page 126 *"There must be…"* The Quote Garden, *Stress Quotes,* www.quotegarden.com/stress.html (Jun. 22, 2009).

Page 126 *Dr. Andrew Weil…* Andrew Weil, *Eight Weeks to Optimum Health, Revised Edition: A Proven Program for Taking Full Advantage of Your Body's Natural Healing Power* (New York: Knopf, 2006).

Page 131 *"Music was…"* ThinkExist.com, *Maya Angelou Quotes,* www.thinkexist.com/quotation/music_was_my_refuge-i_ could_crawl_into_the_space/152801.html (Jun. 22, 2009).

Page 132 *Incorporating music into your life…* American Music Therapy Association, *Music Therapy Makes A Difference,* www.musictherapy.org (Jun. 22, 2009).

Page 132 *Psychological effects of music…* Sarah Ainsworth and Philippa Danks Atilla Szabo, *Experimental Comparison of the Psychological Benefits of Aerobic Exercise, Humor and Music* (Humor, 2005), 18:235-246.

Page 132 *Simply Music…* SimplyMusic.com, *A New World of Learning,* www.simplymusic.com/ (Jun. 22, 2009).

Page 133 *"I think…"* QuotationsPage.com, *George Eliot Shaw Quotes,* www.quotationspage.com/quote/1590.html (Jun. 22, 2009).

Page 134 *Perceived relaxation…* Elise Labbee Jason Burns, Kathryn Williams and Jennifer McCall, *Perceived and Physiological Indicators of Relaxation: As different as Mozart and Alice in Chains* (Applied Psychophysiology and Biofeedback, 1999), 24:197-202.

Page 134 *Road rage… Dwight Hennessy and Brad Totten David Wiesenthal,* The Influence of Music on Driver Stress *(Journal of Applied Social Psychology, 2000), 30:1709-1719.*

Page 138 *Two monologues..."* The Quote Garden, *Speaking Quotes*, www.quotegarden.com/speaking.html (Jun. 22, 2009).

Page 139 *"The problem..."* WisdomQuotes.com, *George Bernard Shaw Quotes*, www.wisdomquotes.com/003139.html (Jun. 22, 2009).

Page 140 *"Self-silenced" women...* Lisa Sullivan Elaine Eaker, Margaret Kelly-Hayes, Ralph D'Agostino and Emelia Benjamin, *Marital Status, Marital Strain, and Risk of Coronary Heart Disease or Total Mortality* (The Framingham O ffspring Study: Psychosomatic Medicine, 2007), 69 (6): 509-513.

Page 142 *David Nokav...* David Novak, *The Education of an Accidental CEO: Lessons Learned from the Trailer Park to the Corner Office* (New York: Crown Business, 2007).

Page 145 *"Change is..."* LeadershipNow.org, *Quotes on Change*, www.leadershipnow.com/changequotes.html (Jun. 22, 2009).

Page 146 *"It is not..."* QuoteWorld.org, *William Deming Quotes*, www.quoteworld.org/quotes/3573 (Jun. 22, 2009).

Page 147 *LifePath...* LifePath LLC, *Healthcare & Change Resilience*, www.ithappens.com/ (Jun. 22, 2009).

Page 147 *When 'It Happiness'...* Julie Smith, *"It" Happens! How to Become Change-Resilient* (Morgantown, WV: Lifepath LLC, 2005).

Page 150 *Montel Williams...* Oprah.com, *Montel Williams' Life With Multiple Sclerosis*, www.oprah.com/printarticlefull/oprahshow/20090305-tows-montel-williams-ms (Jun. 22, 2009).

Page 151 *Steve Jobs...* Stanford News Service, *Text of Steve Jobs' Commencement Address*, www.news.stanford.edu/news/2005/june15/jobs-061505.html (Jun. 22, 2009).

Page 156 *VIA Assessment...* To complete the evaluation yourself, go to www.authentichappiness.sas.upenn.edu/default.aspx or visit www.yourhappinessprescrition.com for a link.

Page 157 *"Happiness is..."* ThinkExist.com, *Ayn Rand Quotes*, www.en.thinkexist.com/quotation/happiness_is_that_state_of_consciousness_which/222646.html (Jun. 22, 2009).

Page 157 *"Success is..."* ThinkExist.com, *Marilyn vos Savant Quotes*, www.en.thinkexist.com/quotation/success_is_achieved_by_developing_our_strengths/183198.html (Jun. 22, 2009).

Page 158 *Oprah...* The Museum of Broadcast Communications, *Winfrey, Oprah*, www.museum.tv/archives/etv/W/htmlW/winfreyopra/winfreyopra.htm (Jun. 22, 2009).

Page 160 *Millard Dean Fuller...* New York Times, Douglas Martin, *Millard Fuller, 74, Who Founded Habitat for Humanity, Is Dead* (Feb. 2, 2009).

Page 160 *"It's not..."* FamousQuotes.com, *Millard Fuller Quotes*, www.famousquotes.com/show/1025319 (Jun. 22, 2009).

Page 163 *The 7 Habits...* Stephen Convey, *The 7 Habits of Highly Effective People* (New York: Free Press, 1990).

Page 164 *"Competition has..."* BrainyQuote.com, *Franklin D. Roosevelt Quotes*, www.brainyquote.com/quotes/authors/f/franklin_d_roosevelt.html (Jun. 22, 2009).

Page 165 *"Conflict is..."* ThinkExist.com, *Max Lucado Quotes*, www.en.thinkexist.com/quotation/conflict_is_inevitable-but_combat_is_optional/14239.html (Jun. 22, 2009).

Page 165 Zappos.com

Page 166 *Tim Ferriss...* Timothy Ferriss, *The 4-Hour Workweek: Escape 9-5, Live Anywhere, and Join the New Rich* (New York: Crown, 2007).

Page 170 *Benefits of spirituality...* Suite101.com, *Health Benefits of Meditation*, www.meditation-health.suite101.com/article.cfm/health_benefits_of_meditation (Jun. 22, 2009).

Page 170 *"The foundations..."* QuoteBlock.com, *Quotation by Ralph Waldo Emerson*, www.quoteblock.com/quote/the-foundations-of-a-person-are-not-in-matter-but (Jun. 22, 2009).

Page 172 *"The purpose..."* Favourite-Famous-Quotes.com, *Life Quotes*, www.favorite-famous-quotes.com/life-quotes.html (Jun. 22, 2009)

Page 173 *The Message...* Peterson, E., The Message: The Bible in Contemporary Language *(NavPress: Colorado Springs, 2002).*

Page 173 *When Bad Things...* Harold Kushner, *When Bad Things Happen to Good People* (New York: Avon, 1983).

Page 173 *Awakening Self-Esteem...* Arthur and Christine Nezu, *Awakening Self-Esteem: Spiritual and Psychological Techniques to Enhance Your Well-Being* (New York: New Harbinger Publications, 2004).

Page 178 *"Declare today..."* QuotesDaddy.com. Oprah Winfrey Quotes, *www.quotesdaddy.com/author/Oprah+Winfrey (Jun. 22, 2009).*

Page 181 *Simpleology...* Simpleology.com, *The Simple Science of Getting What You Want*, www.simpleology.com (Jun. 22, 2009).

Page 183 *Weight gain & sleep...* Atul Malhotra Sanjay Patel, David White, Daniel Gottlieb and Frank Hu, *Association between Reduced Sleep and Weight Gain in Women* (American Journal of Epidemiology, 2006), 15;164(10):947-54.

Page 184 *"No day... "* ThinkExist.com, *Carrie P. Snow Quotes* www.thinkexist.com/quotation/no_day_is_so_bad_it_can-t_be_fixed_with_a_nap/201201.html (Jun. 22, 2009).

Page 186 *Sleeping Pills...* Siri Omvik Børge Sivertsen, Ståle Pallesen, Bjørn Bjorvatn, Odd Havik, Gerd Kvale, Geir Høstmark Nielsen and Inger Hilde Nordhus, *Cognitive Behavioral Therapy vs Zopiclone for Treatment of Chronic Primary Insomnia in Older Adults* (Journal of the American Medical Association, 2006), 295: 2851-2858.

Page 189 *"Thousands of... "* ThinkExist.com, *Buddha Quotes* www.en.thinkexist.com/quotation/thousands_of_candles_can_be_lighted_from_a_single/8680.html (Jun. 22, 2009).

BONUS

Have you ever learned something you think is great — something that could really make a significant difference to you — only to miss out on it due to "life" getting in the way?

It could have been exercise, for example: you might have really got into a good working out routine, but then have stopped because of other commitments. You didn't stop believing that exercise could help you or that it made you feel good, of course — you just stopped making time for it.

Let's not let that happen with your happiness: it's just far too important!

Maybe things would be better if you had your own Personal Happiness Coach — someone to send you reminders, check up on your progress and encourage you to keep going?

I want to be that person — and best of all, I won't cost you a dime.

Sign up now at www.ahappyyou.com/happyyear to get an entire year's FREE happiness coaching tips from me. This will really help you to fulfill your happiness prescription and set you on the path to a happy, satisfying life. Best of all, you can even share this link and my advice with your friends and family.

Let's start a Happiness Revolution!